Stoicism

The Practical Guide to the Stoic Philosophy and Art of Happiness in Modern Life to Help You Develop Your Self-Discipline, Critical Thinking, and Mental Toughness and Live a Better Life

Table of Contents

Chapter 1: Introduction 6

    It Was Built for Hard Times......................... 8

    Stoicism Is Made for Globalization............. 10

    You're Already Part-Stoic............................ 11

    Unofficial Philosophy of the Military.......... 13

    Philosophy for Leadership 13

Chapter 2: What is Stoicism? 16

    The Stoics 18

    The Main Principles of Stoicism 22

Chapter 3: The History of Stoicism 34

    Early Stoa (300 – 100 BC) – Zeno, Cleanthes, and Chrysippus.......................... 35

    Middle Stoa (100 BC – 0) – Panaetius, Posidonius, Cicero, and Cato 37

    Late Stoa (0 – 200 AD) – Seneca, Epictetus, and Aurelius 39

    In Summary... 40

Chapter 4: Stoicism and Happiness 42

    A View From Above 44

    Contemplate the Ideal Man 46

    Cultivating Philanthropy 48

    Self Retreat 50

    The Stripping Method 54

    Negative Visualization 56

    Physical Self-Control Training 59

    Don't Outsource Your Happiness 61

    Forego Ego and Vanity 73

    Stand Your Ground 85

Chapter 5: On Mindfulness Practices 87

    Stoic Mindfulness 87

    Meditation 90

    How to Develop Awareness of Emotions and Thoughts 106

Chapter 6: On Consolidation of Thoughts ... 121

    Philosophical Journal 122

    Early Morning Reflection 124

    Bedtime Reflection 126

    How Journaling Leads to a Better Life 128

Chapter 7: Overcoming Negative Emotions 148

    Stay Focused 148

    Develop an Internal Locus of Control 149

    Guard Your Time 151

    On Trusting the Process 163

    On Dealing with Anger 170

Chapter 8: On the Art of Mental Toughness 180

    Deconstruct Things 182

    Reframe Negative Events 184

    Acknowledge Your Challenges 186

    Find Your Purpose 188

    Recharge and Recover 190

    Flex the Muscle 192

    Stay Resilient 194

Chapter 9: Other Practical Tips and Practices 195

   Add a Reserve Clause – If Nothing Prevents You 195

   Love Your Fate 197

   Forgive the Wrongs of Others 199

   Buy Tranquility 201

   16 Lessons for Living 202

Chapter 10: Conclusion 208

Chapter 1: Introduction

Stoicism is intended to teach us all of how unpredictable the real world can be, and how brief our life is. It teaches us how to maintain mental resilience during hardship and how to be in control of your own emotions. Finally, it addresses the dissatisfaction that lies in our impulsive dependency on reflexive senses rather than logic.

Stoicism does not discuss complicated theories of what the world should be. It merely acknowledges that the world is random and flawed, and advises us to accept it as it is. It focuses on helping us overcome our destructive emotions as a reaction to what the world throws at us, and compels us to act on what can be acted on. Stoicism is practical, built for action, not an endless debate of what should be. It is about sticking your nose into the grindstone and getting things done. But how relevant is Stoicism in modern day society?

Well, let us take a look at Clinton's line on Obama. He struck a familiar chord because he reminded us of another politician known for his coolness. That person is Cato the Younger.

Cato was a practitioner of Stoicism, which was an ancient Greek religion that he brought with him to Rome. It's not that Obama was a Stoic, but we can see the public's response to his self-control. It shows how poorly Stoic qualities can go over in our time. Stoicism was built on emotional control, which seems alien in the age where everyone is sharing everything.

It is a shame, actually. We can learn so much from it, especially when every little thing screams for our attention and tries to control how we should think and feel. Moreover, the Stoic legacy has shaped our world more than you think. There are five main reasons why Stoicism matters nowadays more than ever:

It Was Built for Hard Times

Hard times create strong people. Strong people create good times. Good times create weak people. Weak people create hard times. The cycle goes on.

Stoicism came around as the world was falling apart. Birthed in Athens a few decades after Alexander the Great's conquests and premature death, Stoicism took off mainly because it gave the people security and pace during the time of war and crisis. Stoicism did not promise material security or peace in the afterlife. However, it did promise unshakable happiness in this life.

Stoicism reminds us that we cannot secure our happiness if we base it on changeable, destructible things. Our careers can grow and wilt, the number on our bank account can rise and fall. Even our loved ones can be taken from us one way or another. So, it is clear that you cannot build a foundation of happiness on external things. There is one thing that the world cannot change. That is our inner selves, our choice to behave in a specific way, to be reasonable, and to be virtuous.

The world can take everything from us. Come what may. Stoicism reminds us that we have a fortress on the inside. Epictetus was born a slave and crippled at a very young age. He wrote, "here is the good? In the will... If anyone is unhappy, let him remember that he is unhappy by reason of himself alone."

It's a natural instinct to cry out in pain, but the Stoics suggest that we stay indifferent to everything that happens outside, and remain equally happy both in time of abundance and scarcity. That is not to say that Stoicism is easy to adopt into your life, but it at least offers us freedom from passion, which is the freedom from the emotions that have controlled our words and actions for a very long time. A real Stoic does feel emotions, but he or she knows how to master their emotions. Stoicism recognizes that emotions such as grief, fear, or greed only enter our mind when we permit them.

A teaching like this seems to be designed for a world on edge, whether it's the chaotic world of ancient Greece or in a modern financial crisis. Then again, Epictetus said that as long as we place our happiness on perishable things, our worlds will always be on edge.

Stoicism Is Made for Globalization

The world in which Stoicism was born is from a parochial and xenophobic world in which people cling to an age-old division of nationality, religion, and status. Openly embracing those divisions may not be an easy task, but Stoicism encourages us to do so. It was one of the first Western philosophies to preach universal brotherhood. Epictetus said that everyone has ownership of the world we live in. We are all members of the great city of gods and men. Marcus Aurelius, the Roman emperor, as history's well-known Stoic, reminded himself that he loves the world as much as he loves his own people.

If the key to our happiness is in our own will, then even the greatest social dividers seem insignificant. Seneca lived a life of slavery, but he urged others to "remember that those who call you a slave came from the same stock, are smiled upon by the same skies, and on equal terms with yourself breathe, live, and die."

This embrace of world-city, where everyone is of one nation and race, made Stoicism the ideal philosophy for the Roman Empire. This brought together people from different races and religions. Therefore, Stoicism is relevant in a globalized world.

You're Already Part-Stoic

This has been taught in many religions that humans are under the same creator, God himself. He tells us to moderate and master our impulses rather than giving into them. Of course, we are humans, so we will probably fail this mission. This may sound familiar in your religion because the idea behind this religious philosophy is Stoicism.

Christianity is a deeply Stoic religion. After all, Stoicism dominated Roman culture for centuries. From there, Christianity went mainstream in the same culture. Moreover, many early leaders of the Christian church were former Stoics. So, we know that Christianity borrowed much of its thought and terminology from Stoicism.

Unfortunately, as time went on, church leaders, who wanted to emphasize the uniqueness of their faith, started to downplay the Stoic connection. But we do know that Stoicism was at the foundation of the Christian religion.

Unofficial Philosophy of the Military

Back in 1965, James Stockdale's a-4E Skyhawk was shot down over Vietnam and he was held as a prisoner of war for seven years without receiving any prisoner rights. We will discuss his life in more details in a later chapter, but he drew strength and determination from Stoicism and survived imprisonment. It helped him confront the grim reality of the situation without giving in to despair and depression. This is what a soldier, student, and office workers alike need to keep in mind their entire life.

Philosophy for Leadership

Stoicism reminds us not to control things outside our control. Instead, we should strive to control ourselves first. We should not try to exert influence over the world that is always changing as we will be subject to disappointment and failure. Ever since Marcus

Aurelius, world leaders have discovered that a Stoic attitude still gets them respect in the face of failure and prevents them from being arrogant in the face of success.

Stoicism gives us courage in the face of uncertainty. Leaders, especially, are subject to risk and change, so it is not surprising to see that many leaders find the philosophy of Stoicism appealing for their mental health. You can see this in Barack Obama's many public appearances and interviews. He displayed a Stoic demeanor.

In short, Stoicism does not guarantee success, but it does guarantee happiness no matter what situation you are in. It guides you on a path of virtue and gives you a realistic view of leading your life.

This is what this book intends to do: introduce you to the ideas of Stoicism and give you practical exercises you can incorporate into your life. Without further ado, let us get into this.

Chapter 2: What is Stoicism?

Stoicism is basically designed to help individuals lead their best possible lives. It is a philosophy of life that aims to minimize negative emotions and maximize positive ones. Not only that, but it also paves the way for individuals to hone their virtues of character.

Stoicism gives us a framework so we can find order within the chaos of life. This is applicable at any stage of your life, and in many situations. It gives us a sense of purpose by reminding us of what is really important and giving us practical strategies to get more of what is valuable.

Stoicism was created with the intention to be useful, actionable, and understandable. Practicing it is a lot easier than you think, as it does not require any learning nor does it involve meditation for extended periods of time. Here, we focus on methods that are more immediate, useful, and practical so you can achieve tranquility and improve your strength of character.

Stoicism is a school of philosophy with its source tracing back to ancient Greece and Rome in the early 3rd century.

Here, we would like to point out the differences in peoples' thought processes back then. You see, the Stoics provided amazing and compelling answers to questions about our troubles, fear, stress, and anxiety. Ask a friend what does he or she want out of life? Many people cannot answer such an open-ended question, but the Stoics can, and they may offer an operating system that deals with the trials of the human condition.

Whatever it is that people want, it all boils down to happiness and peace of mind that comes not from wealth or titles, but rather by being a virtuous person.

For example, an individual can hone their virtues of character by giving more value on actions instead of words. Basically, positive behavior creates a more positive life experience. The opposite is also true.

In short, stoicism was an ancient school of philosophy that guided us to a more virtuous life, maximizing happiness and reducing negative emotions. Its values have been tried and tested throughout human history by famous individuals such as George Washington, Arianna Huffington, Tim Ferriss, Thomas Jefferson, and many more.

While its guiding principles were established long ago, the stoic's strategies are even more important today than they were in ancient times. Our lives are more chaotic than they were a few centuries ago. So, stoicism is forever relevant to us.

The Stoics

Stoicism was not established by the hands of Zeno alone. There are many thinkers that helped form the Stoic philosophy. They are:

Zeno of Citium

The stoic philosophy was founded by Zeno of Citium. He turned his misfortune in the form of a shipwreck that left him stranded in Athens into an opportunity by capitalizing on all the philosophical resources in the city. He attended all lectures from other schools of philosophy such as Cynicism and Epicureanism and then created his own philosophy. The word Stoicism came from the word "stōïkos," which refers to the Stoa Poikile (a renounced painted porch in Athens) from which Zeno preached his theory.

Marcus Aurelius

Marcus Aurelius, being one of the most influential individuals in our history, was the head of the Roman Empire for two decades. He ruled the empire when it was one of the largest and most influential civilizations in the world.

While Aurelius had limitless power, he could do whatever he pleased on a whim with impunity. However, he practiced and lived the Stoic philosophy instead.

As you have already guessed, living a stoic life was not easy. He documented his struggles to lead a restrained, wise, and virtuous life. It was only much later that his personal writings were discovered, collected, and then published under a book titled "Meditations." This is now one of the masterpieces and go-to documents if you wish to know more about stoicism. Aurelius wrote about his own thoughts and practical approaches toward stoicism, strategies you can incorporate into your life to help you cope with stressful situations.

Lucius Annaeus Seneca

Lucius Annaeus Seneca had a remarkable charisma and a solver's tongue thanks to his occupation as a statesman, a dramatist, and a writer. He had a colorful, straightforward, and entertaining way of describing Stoicism. Thanks to his simplistic approach to teaching stoicism, we recommend that you check out his works if you are new. Moreover, Seneca's thoughts are more relatable for modern audiences because his thoughts are more relevant to us, covering topics such as friendship, mortality, altruism, and the proper use of time.

Epictetus

Epictetus was once a slave, but his life eventually improved to the point that he became one of the most analytical thinkers of Stoicism. You can find practical strategies to implement stoicism into your life in his handbook titled "The Enchiridion." He had a knack for explaining how stoicism can improve a person's life dramatically and made a compelling case for why everyone should consider making stoicism their primary operating system. Many of his teachings are, though recognizable, tragically uncredited.

The Main Principles of Stoicism

Initially, Stoicism focused mainly on logic and physics. As time went on, it shifted to more psychological concerns such as wellbeing and tranquility. While the Stoics can never convene to affirm all of their tenants precisely, they all agree on certain principles that form the core of stoicism.

Most importantly, these principles are not just something that you can think about momentarily and then forget about. They should be practiced every day of your life.

Walk the Talk

"Waste no more time arguing what a good man should be. Be one." – Marcus Aurelius

What does this tell us? We as Stoics should not concern ourselves with worthless and purely theoretical contemplation. Focus on real-world pragmatism instead of pondering just for the sake of it.

Expanding on the idea of pragmatism, in the real world, you need to find answers and act on them. Being a true Stoic is not just about being an armchair philosopher who just rambles on and on about theories. You need to walk the talk, so to speak. Be the person who says what should be done and gets things done.

Moreover, you may notice that the Stoics also have a concern of leading a righteous life. Of course, we have already established that this principle includes taking action and not wasting time pondering what should be. Stoics believe that a good life is one of moral action. So, if you want to live well, be a morally just person.

Control Only What You Can

"The chief task in life is simply this: to identify and separate matters so that I can say clearly to myself which are externals not under my control, and which have to do with the choices I actually control. Where then do I look for good and evil? Not to uncontrollable externals, but within myself to the choices that are my own…" – Epictetus

In the previous section, we discussed only needing to worry about what we can actually control. If we wish to worry, there are so many things to worry about. Global tension over North Korea, the South China Sea, and global warming are three of the major things out there. The Stoics understand that everyone has no control over everything, even the big guys out there. You cannot control most of what happens in life. If anything, worrying about things outside your realm of control is unproductive, and may irritate you. This prevents you from reaching mental tranquility, which is one of the most important things in a Stoic's life.

In the face of all of these troublesome events, we should all be able to differentiate between what is within our control, what we should worry about, and the things that are not. If you cannot control something, no one will think less of you if you ignore it. After all, there is no point in wasting energy over uncontrollable events. So, whereas others worry and fuss about things they cannot change, the Stoics focus their energy on finding creative solutions instead of on the problems themselves.

Be Grateful

"No person has the power to have everything they want, but it is in their power not to want what they don't have, and to cheerfully put to good use what they have." – Seneca

Epictetus lived a life of slavery without personal possessions. Even his own body was not his. He hit rock bottom, yet he pursued the

Stoic life anyways. Of course, while it focuses more on peace of mind, that does not mean you must forego all material possessions. In fact, the Stoics believe that these possessions serve to increase your happiness and improve your ability to lead a virtuous life. However, be very careful about the hype and power of consumerism that would invade your tranquility of mind and decision-making. Many of us are upset at the things we cannot have. Maybe your neighbor has a more beautiful, expensive car. Perhaps your boss has a kinder and more beautiful spouse. You may overlook the fact that you are in better health or have fewer problems to worry about.

Another example of poverty is Seneca. He would fast and wear unfashionable clothing to remind himself that people do not need material possessions to live a good life. They are good to have, but not necessary for your peace of mind. In all, almost every one of us has enough to get by and be happy. Still, we are upset about our lives because we keep maintaining our insatiable desire for more.

There is a difference between want and need. Need refers to material things we require to survive, including food, shelter, clothing, etc. These physiological needs are located at the bottom of Maslow's needs hierarchy, meaning that these things are a must-have for survival. You do not need much else from other levels to achieve happiness. On the other hand, want is something we feel that we need, but is actually not necessary for us. If we can live or work without it, then it is probably something you want, not need.

So, what do we learn from this? Stoics try not to suffer over what they do not have. Instead, they focus on being grateful for what they currently have.

Be Positive

"I judge you unfortunate because you have never lived through misfortune. You have passed through life without an opponent – no one can ever know what you are capable of, not even you." – Seneca

The Stoics have a different view of misfortune. We see it as a tragic incident or a coincidence that does not favor us. They expect mishaps to happen, as they often will, but they use them to hone their virtues instead of mourning about it. Of course, that does not mean that they are happy when they are struck with misfortune. They just try not to lament about it as it changes nothing. Instead, they strive to develop their own character through hardships whenever possible.

For instance, suppose that you got into a road accident and broke both your legs. You need to be hospitalized and bed-ridden for months until they heal. Any normal human being would adopt the "woe is me" mentality and be grumpy for the rest of their recovery phase. Stoics, on the other hand, do not dwell on their misfortune and instead use the time they now have (because they do not have to work) to do something productive. That can be reading books, writing, etc. They try to reframe the event as a means for personal growth.

In short, Stoics do not let adverse events ruin their peace of mind. Instead, they try to make the most out of the situation.

Respond Differently

"External things are not the problem. It's your assessment of them. Which you can erase right now." – Marcus Aurelius

The Stoic way of life has found its way into modern psychology. For instance, the famous Cognitive Behavioral Therapy (CBT) is based on the concept that our thoughts (cognition), feelings (emotion), and actions (behavior) are all interconnected. It goes like this: thoughts influence feelings and feelings influence behavior. Now we know that modern psychological science proves that Stoicism works.

In many ways, our thoughts determine how we experience reality. For instance, one person may be a nervous wreck when asked to sing on the stage, whereas the other person would grab the microphone and hop right on to the beat. For two people who experience the same hardship, how they assess the situation determines how they feel and behave.

The best way to achieve psychological wellbeing, one should monitor their own inner critic towards greater optimism. Remember that it is not the event itself that creates a negative experience, it is how you perceive it.

Put Effort In Everything You Do

"Let us prepare our minds as if we'd come to the very end of life. Let us postpone anything. Let us postpone anything. Let us balance life's books each day... The one who puts the finishing touches on their life each day is never short of time." – Seneca

"Keep death and exile before your eyes each day, along with everything that seems terrible – by doing so, you'll never have a base thought nor will you have excessive desire." – Epictetus

In many philosophies, "Memento Mori" is an important concept for both the Stoics and the Existentialists. It basically means "remember that you will die," Morbid? Probably. But this is the stark reality that we all have to acknowledge. Our time on this planet is but a fleeting moment. Seneca and Epictetus understood this very well as they firmly believed that contemplating one's mortality can compel one to be grateful and take more virtuous actions.

By reminding ourselves of our inevitable demise, we learn to appreciate what we have while we still have it. Even with few material possessions, you can still appreciate the good health and wellbeing you have, while you still have them.

By keeping in mind the fact that you are not immortal, you tend to have a better idea of what really matters. The whole idea can be simplified into one short advice: You could get hit by a bus tomorrow. Morbid?True. Still, the point this advice is trying to make is that you should live today as if it's your last day. We all have things to worry about but don't fuss about the small things.

Virtue is Paramount

It is worth repeating the fact that Stoics should only concern themselves with the question of virtue. The excellence of character is more important than wealth, or even health. The Stoics believe that so long as they behave and think virtuously, there is no need to concern themselves with the influence of external events that they cannot control. Whether or not people are impolite or you experience a series of unfortunate events, it does not matter. What matters is that you respond in a virtuous way. If you do, you are leading a good life.

Chapter 3: The History of Stoicism

In the previous chapter, we looked at some of the greatest Stoic philosophers and how exactly they contributed to Stoicism in summary. Here, we will study these ancient Stoic philosophers in depth.

For the Stoics, the ultimate goal of our life is "Eudaimonia," which is a state of contentment and flourishing. This can be achieved by living in accordance with nature, as all animals should. Living with nature entails fulfilling your role in the cosmos which is related to the notions of fate and providence and living as a human. Since we are different from animals because we have the capacity for reasoning, we must use this capacity to act accordingly.

Basically, we must act rationally and not be led around by our passion. External circumstances should be viewed objectively, as in neither good nor bad. Therefore, it is best that we are indifferent to them. The entire point of Eudaimonia and the methods to reach it have been developed over the course of human history. Here, we will go briefly over the golden era of stoicism, which is between 300 BC and 200 AD. We will divide this time into three periods: the early, middle, and late stoa. Because the only source in existence about stoicism only dates back to the late stoa period. This is the most well-known of them all.

Early Stoa (300 – 100 BC) – Zeno, Cleanthes, and Chrysippus

The school of stoicism was founded by Zeno of Citium around 300 BC in Athens. He opposed the school of Epicureanism, which was popular back then. It was founded by Epicurus, who held a more materialistic view of the world. He believed in an accidental nature and a materialistic world, driven only by pain and pleasure. In contrast, Zeno developed his own school of stoicism, which was inspired by many other schools such as Cynicism. Zeno prioritized virtue and simplicity. After recovering from the shipwreck and attending lectures from great philosophers of his time, he started teaching from the Stoa Poikile at the center of Athens. This stoa was a covered colonnade and publicly assessable. From this name, Zeno found the name of his philosophy. Zeno laid the foundation of stoicism and had a powerful influence in the school. He continued maintaining the distinction of the stoic philosophy in three main areas: ethics, physics, and logic. Today, stoicism emphasizes the most on ethics, even though Zeno argued that ethics should always be supported by logic and physics.

Zeno was succeeded by Cleanthes, his pupil, who added a little teaching of his own in addition to following Zeno's teachings. The next leader of the school of stoicism was Chrysippus of Soli, who contributed a lot to the school. He further developed the three parts of philosophy (ethics, physics, and logic). By solidifying and expanding what Zeno had taught, Chrysippus made sure that stoicism was one of the strongest philosophies in history. After that, the school was led by Zeno of Tarsus, Diogenes of Babylon, and Antipater of Tarsus.

Middle Stoa (100 BC – 0) – Panaetius, Posidonius, Cicero, and Cato

Around 100 BC, stoicism began to shift from Athens to Rhodos and Rome. The seventh scholar, Panaetius, was more flexible in his beliefs than Zeno, who was strict. His contribution was in the form of the simplification of the stoic ideas on physics. He was not as interested in logic in the school of stoicism. This shifted the stoic philosophy closer to Neoplatonism, not to mention making it more assessable to the public. He also brought Stoicism to Rome. Panaetius is considered to be the last scholar because the middle stoa was more elastic, as well as the differences in opinions. After that, there was no longer a unified and undisputed school of stoicism. Still, the Stoic philosophy proves to be able to withstand the test of time as it is more relevant than ever.

Posidonius further reinforced Panaetius' ideas and moved stoicism even closer to Plato and Aristotle, which could be considered to be a Neoplatonist. In Rome, Cicero, and Cato the younger adopted stoicism. Cato, known for his uncompromising moral integrity and his austere way of life, is considered to be the symbol of absolute morality and stoicism. He seems to be associated closer to the teachings of Zeno and Chrysippus than the more flexible philosophy of Panaetius and Posidonius.

Late Stoa (0 – 200 AD) – Seneca, Epictetus, and Aurelius

During the Roman imperial period, the Stoic philosophers were primarily interested in the questions of ethics. Logics and physics did not receive as much attention anymore. We know much from stoicism from the late stoa as their original writings have survived until today. One of these writings is from Seneca, who used the uniqueness of day-to-day situations to discuss moral issues. Seneca was widely praised for his personalized writing on the school of philosophy and his book Epistulae is still widely known today. If you wish to start studying Stoicism, we recommend you read Epictetus' handbook. Epictetus was born a slave and provided many insights into stoicism. On the other spectrum, we have Marcus Aurelius who was the Roman emperor. His most prominent work is Ta Eis Heauton (To himself), which he wrote as a personal journal during his military campaign in

Germania. Now, it is published under the title "Meditations." This book is the most read and it discussed stoicism extensively, not to mention inspiring people around the world to this day. Concepts such as self-discipline, reason, and world citizenship are still relevant today. Meditations are also used as the main source of personal improvement and growth, arousing renewed interest in stoicism recently. This book is considered to be the last major work from the late stoa.

In Summary

In short, stoicism has a long history and it withstood the test of time. From great philosophers such as Zeno, all the way to Marcus Aurelius, this school of philosophy has developed well and proven itself to be useful and timeless. It is useful for people from all walks of life, from slaves to emperors. It served Epictetus (a slave) and Marcus (an emperor) well, so this philosophy applies to everyone. While the foundation of Stoicism remained the same, the middle stoa changed it from the eccentric to the eclectic. In the end, the late stoa writers such as Epictetus and Marcus Aurelius gave us many indispensable insights into stoicism.

Chapter 4: Stoicism and Happiness

Zeno of Cyprus, the founder of Stoicism, was shipwrecked and stranded in Athens. Back then, and even now, this is considered to be a very unfortunate incident. Unlike us, he did not have access to help or much of anything else. For him, it was a devastating incident which could have been the end of his life. Despite that, he remained unfazed. He did not expect anything good to happen.

After losing everything and now not having much else to do, he simply wandered into a bookshop. There, he found the teaching of Socrates that captivated him instantly. After that, he studied with many great philosophers of his time and decided to impart his wisdom on those who wished to learn from him.

This is where the philosophy of stoicism was born. His wisdom was so well-received that both slaves and kings alike implemented it into their lives. He once joked that he made a prosperous voyage when he suffered shipwreck.

However, stoicism does not end there, as a simple footnote in history. Even centuries later, the philosophy remains more relevant than ever in modern society. If anything, life nowadays is even more chaotic than it once was hundreds of years ago. Therefore, there is no better way to find order within chaos than by starting to simplify things in our lives. In this chapter, we will discuss some of the ways you can achieve happiness through practical exercises. You can implement these seamlessly into your life and they are useful for both Stoics and non-stoics alike.

What we will cover here is not some strange ritual, either. It does not involve spirituality. We focus on simple habits to increase your happiness without the use of any equipment.

A View From Above

This activity is intended to stop your worries by reminding you how insignificant you really are in the grand scheme of things. There is no way you can mess things up that badly on that scale. In other words, this activity helps you to see the bigger picture. Basically, you use your imagination to try and see yourself from a distant standpoint.

There are a few ways you can do this:

Meditation

There are many forms of meditation, and some people even do it for extended periods of time. However, we want to focus on the activity being practical. Just by meditating for five to ten minutes will suffice. We will cover meditation and mindfulness in the next chapter.

Do It Yourself

This can be a better alternative as it does not require the use of any equipment. You can do it anywhere. However, for the best experience, we recommend you visit the park or beach. To give yourself the magnitude of the whole universe and how insignificant you are in relation to it, you can start by visualizing a bird's eye view from the sky, or much further to a distant nebula if you wish. From that viewpoint, work your way down. For example, if you start from the sky, then come closer to the world and the people living in it. Observe everything that happens, such as first kisses, discoveries, wars, learning, traffic jams, artistic creations, etc. Observe them as they happen, but refrain yourself from judging them. Remember that many of the things you think are important are actually relatively important. Some care about it, some don't. The same can be said about you. You are only relatively important. Some care about you, others do not.

If you wish to take it a step further, you can imagine yourself in a world frozen in time. Imagine yourself walking through this world and how still everything is. Observe and enjoy that moment of stillness and tranquility.

Alternatively, you can imagine yourself at a different point in time. Imagine life in the medieval era, or in the futuristic era. This can help you remember the fact that you did not exist at a certain point in time and, at some point in the future, you will not exist.

Contemplate the Ideal Man

This activity is intended to give you motivation for change to become an ideal individual – the best you. Because we can never become perfect, you can only improve upon yourself gradually.

For this exercise, think about the qualities that an ideal person would have. To help your visualization, let us assume that the Roman and Greek status represent the ideal person. Of course, we will not focus on the physical manifestation, but instead the psychological aspects.

What qualities make a person ideal? In many ways, this is a difficult question to answer. It can be easier to instead focus on what an ideal person would do in the situation. From the actions they take, we can then determine their inner qualities. Hopefully, we can start to emulate them. Of course, an ideal person is nothing more than an image, but our goal here is to strive to be as close to that person as possible.

You can solidify the effectiveness of this exercise further by creating a list of real role models, past or present. Then, conduct a thorough analysis of all those individuals to find the qualities that make them ideal. Find the best qualities, and discard the rest.

Alternatively, you can learn the virtues of an ideal individual by knowing what not to do. You just contemplate the actions of the worst type of person imaginable, and then just avoid being that person.

Cultivating Philanthropy

Before we get into the exercise, let us define philanthropy. It is the desire to promote the welfare of others. Contrary to popular belief, money is not the only means to become a philanthropist. In reality, anyone can be one. All that is needed is the right attitude towards others.

The problem is that we believe that we live in a series of spheres, one inside another. Think of the famous Russian Babushka doll. Each sphere represents a larger distance from our real selves.

So, how do you cultivate philanthropy? The goal here is to bring everyone closer, therefore, merging all of these spheres or layers together. Consider your family to be an extension of yourself. Think of your neighbors as your family. That way, you cultivate a virtue of caring for others, which is key to a virtuous life.

This requires a major change in perspective and it will take a lot of effort. It does have its advantages though. First and most importantly, you will not become overly attached to any particular individual. This prevents you from being devastated in case of loss of friends or their death. Another benefit here is that you will have a larger circle of friends. This exposes you to more culture and viewpoints, meaning the greater the opportunity for learning.

In addition to considering others to be closer to you, there are other things you can do to cultivate the philanthropist within you. You can strike up a pleasant conversation with a stranger, or let your close friend know that you consider them to be a part of your family and that they can and should rely on you.

Self Retreat

Many of us have very good reasons why we would like to travel the world. The most common reason is "to escape and disappear." This is to say that we want to go somewhere where we feel disconnected from the troubles and stress of our everyday routines. So, you may find the idea of a beach in a remote tropical area appealing if you live in the city or you think the bright and colorful lights of the city strikes your fancy better if you live in a remote area. You take yourself to a place where nothing reminds you of your worries. You can achieve peace of mind this way, but this is deeply unphilosophical. You do not need to take a month's vacation and spend a hundred thousand dollars at a remote island to experience mental tranquility. Peace of mind and freedom are some of the things that come from within. If you run away from what troubles you, you are running away from yourself. Unfortunately, you cannot run away from yourself.

There is a cheaper way to find mental tranquility. Instead of traveling outside your country to some remote location, just travel inside your mind, especially if you need peace of mind or freedom. The freest place is inside your own mind. You can choose to be different right here and now. There is no need to travel to find yourself. All you need is about ten minutes a day to shut the outside world out and allow yourself to look inside your own mind.

"People seek retreats for themselves in the countryside, by the seashore, in the hills, and you too have made it your habit to long for that above all else. But this is altogether unphilosophical, when it is possible for you to retreat into yourself whenever you please; for nowhere can one retreat into greater peace or freedom from care than within one's own soul, especially when a person has things within him that he merely has to look at to recover from that moment of perfect ease of mind (and by ease of mind I mean nothing other than having one's mind in good order). So constantly, grant yourself this retreat and so renew yourself; but keep within you concise and basic precepts that will be enough, at first encounter, to cleanse you from all distress and to send you back without discontent of the life to which you will return." – Marcus Aurelius

There was a video about a prisoner who was sentenced to prison for life. Realizing that he would spend the rest of his days locked in a cell, he started discussing how he could escape it. Not by breaking out, of course. He had a more philosophical pursuit and so he started reading and thinking. After all, since this was his life now, he might as well make use of the time he had left to work on becoming a better person. Now, he does not let the four walls of his cell trap his mind. But what about us? Our body is free, but can we say the same for our mind? It is possible that every one of us is mentally trapped in some way. Some are depressed, for instance.

There are a few things you should keep in mind when you want to go on a self retreat. First, know that your experiences of the events are dictated by how you feel about them, not by the events themselves. Second, know that everything is changing all the time, so there is no point in stressing about it because you cannot do anything about it anyway. Finally, your life is limited, so there is no point fussing all the time.

Other than just retreating into your mind, we have two other activities you should try out. Now, if you have a hard time getting inside your own head, you can visit Calm.com. The website has tools you can use to help you relax before starting this journey. If you want to make this challenging, you can try and practice self retreat in non-ideal situations. It can be when you are watching TV with someone else or perhaps taking the journey while in public transport.

The Stripping Method

Every single situation has many layers, similar to an onion. To get to the heart of the problem, you need to peel away these layers, which are the things that we bring to the situation, not the issue itself. You can only act according to an ethical framework only when you consider the core issues without the unimportant layers. What does that mean?

Simply put, when you need to solve a problem, you focus on getting the job done. Don't consider your reputation or whatever personal advantage you think you can get out of it. So, ask yourself a few questions.

"What value does this situation bring to everyone?" In many cases, the answer is "none."

"What type of qualities does this situation require?" If you check all of the boxes, then great! If not, then use this situation as an opportunity to develop them.

For instance, many of us struggle in finding a direction in life as we are growing up. We do not really know what we want to do with our lives. We may have some faint ideas, but we still do not feel that we should pursue them. If we strip this question down to its core, we are lost not mainly because we do not know what we can do that would be fulfilling and meaningful. We are struggling to find meaning in our lives. Meaningful pursuits do not always involve monetization, although you may find the perfect career if it is meaningful and you feel passionate about it and can monetize it.

We have already established that material possessions should only serve to further enhance your peace of mind. You do not need them to achieve mental tranquility. When finding meaningful pursuits, you should disregard wealth, title, and other's expectations. That way, you won't be dragged into leading a life that is far from who you really are.

So, ask yourself what you would do if money is not something you need to worry about. Be honest with yourself when answering this question and then go and do that.

Negative Visualization

Before we get into this, we need to understand what Hedonic Adaptation is. It is the phenomenon in which we get used to the things we have and then start to take them for granted. For instance, when you buy a new phone, you treat it as if it is a fragile object. You would not even dare to drop it from a centimeter high. After having it for a year, you would not even think twice about throwing it across the room into your bed. This also applies to your relationships, which makes Hedonic Adaptation very dangerous.

For instance, a couple falls madly in love with each other and gets married. Everyone can see how much they love each other. They are inseparable. Even when they are not together, they send sweet, romantic texts back and forth ceaselessly. All is good, until about five years into the relationship. They are not together as often, and even when they are, they do not talk to each other much, let alone show signs of affection. The texts are few and far between. Eventually, they divorce. This is the effect of Hedonic Adaptation in a relationship. That is not to say that every single relationship follows this route, but we want to point out what happens if you do not maintain it. Certain things may be important to you, but after a few months or years, they don't seem to be as relevant. That is how we feel. Until we lose it again, do we understand just how much something is worth to us.

So, how do we combat Hedonic Adaptation? Through negative visualization.

Negative visualization is an exercise intended to remind us of how lucky we are even with what little we have. As the name suggests, you just have to think about the bad things that have happened or the good things that have not. You can also decide the scale of the event:

- Losing all your possessions
- Never having met your soulmate
- The death of a loved one
- Losing a limb(s), sight, or hearing

You can also think about how things will go wrong as you are about to do them. You may argue that this kind of pessimistic thinking is counterintuitive to a happy and peaceful life. In reality, it can greatly alter your perspective. You suddenly become happy with the things that you have and all the bad things that did not happen.

If you are not faint-hearted, you can try and imagine how things could go very wrong when you are doing or about to do them. If you are traveling by plane, imagine that it will malfunction and crash. If that is too morbid, consider imagining having been born in the past era when all the things you take for granted had not been invented yet, and how you would miss them.

Physical Self-Control Training

This exercise is to discipline our mind by purposefully going through physical hardships and going without the things we enjoy. You can say that this is a practical version of negative visualization because you put yourself through the hardship. This training has two purposes:

- To prepare ourselves for physical hardships well in advance or for when we suddenly lose everything
- To train ourselves not to yearn for things that are outside our control. Remember, we can only control our own thoughts and actions.

Remember that you should always grasp everything you get in life loosely. Never become too attached to anything as you may lose it one day. Think of sand. You cannot hold sand tightly because it will slip between your fingers and escape your grasp. So, you can subject yourself through physical self-control training by:

- Not eating anything for a period of time
- Going out in the rainy weather without an umbrella
- For a week, change something in your daily routine to make your day less convenient, straightforward, or uncomfortable
- Try to survive without the internet for a period of time (It's harder than you think!)

It is best to view everything as transient. Everything you own, and even you, will no longer exist one day. You become less attached to your own car if you borrowed it from someone. So, see everything as if it was on a loan. When you lose something, tell yourself that you have not lost it. Instead, say that you have given it back.

Don't Outsource Your Happiness

"I have often wondered how it is that every man loves himself more than all the rest of men, but yet sets less value on his own opinions of himself than on the opinions of others." – Marcus Aurelius

Many things that we do stem from the fact that we want to be liked and accepted. This is because we are social creatures so socializing and being accepted are important to us. These primal needs guide our actions and are often the sole reason why people fall into depression. Disapproval from our social group makes us feel incompetent and detached. Back then, this could result in exile and eventual death in the wilderness. Today, it still holds true. How much time and effort do you spend trying to appeal to others? What does that cost us?

You may be familiar with this quote, "We spend money we don't have, to buy things we don't need, to impress people we don't like." Let's be real here. We all want others to perceive us in a positive light. So, our career and lifestyle choices are based on how we want others to see us rather than what we really want or what is best for us. This is one of the reasons why we all are prisoners in our own mind.

We mentioned earlier in the book that we should only focus on things that we can control. This is what we should strive for. To appeal to everyone is to appeal to no one. You cannot control what others think of you, no matter how hard you try. So, why care about them at all? The Roman statesman Cato led a life that was independent of the opinions of others. So, what did he do? He threw caution to the wind and wore the most hideous and outlandish outfits, and walked around barefooted. Of course, the public reacted negatively, throwing shame and profanity at him. He remained steadfast. It was his way of accustoming himself to be ashamed so that he could endure it when he was ridiculed when he deserved it. It was also his way of despising all sorts of disgrace because he knew what they felt like.

Through this, Cato was able to stand up to Julius Caesar, whom he believed to have too much power. By subjecting himself to public shaming, he honed his mental resilience and was able to make big decisions when they counted, without the fear of disapproval.

We can learn much from him. It is much better for us to live our own lives, on our own terms, and ignore the opinions of others. So, never outsource your happiness.

On the Pursuit of Status

Even though he had composed many famous pieces, the French philosopher Denis Diderot spent a large portion of his life in poverty. Unlike many of us, and similar to many other Enlightenment thinkers of his time, Diderot did not care for material possessions. That was until he received a brand new scarlet robe as a gift from his friend.

The robe was absolutely beautiful, so much so that Diderot treasured it above everything else. However, he realized that the robe was so out of place with everything else in his home. Only his robe was this grand, and he had no other objects to match.

So, what did he do? He went on to replace everything that he owned. His straw chair was replaced with a leather one. A large mirror now took over the mantle of his fireplace. A writing desk now occupied the vacant corner of his house. As you might have guessed, Diderot went into debt very quickly. In his essay titled "Regrets for My Old Dressing Gown," he said that he was the absolute master of his old robe. But now, he had become the slave of the new one.

His misfortune gave the name to a phenomenon known as the Diderot Effect. From what we learned from Diderot, we can say that the acquisition of a new possession is not a singular event. It always leads to more and more. Every single new purchase creates a spiral of consumption that just pushes you to buy more things.

The Diderot Effect

The Diderot Effect is a social phenomenon that points out much of what modern consumerism has become. Many savvy marketers tend to bundle products up together, which happen to complement each other and then sell them to us at a price so compelling that it is nigh impossible to refuse.

A single purchase can lead to many, many bad purchase decisions.

Diderot showed us what would happen if we followed up an innocent purchase with many mindless purchases. Still, it is difficult to suppress this consumption pattern. We are only scratching the surface here. We need to examine Diderot's misfortune closely if we want to understand our true challenge.

In his essay, Diderot did not care much for material possessions until he got the new robe. Initially, he did not see how they represent the inherent value and worth of a person. This is what he wrote:

> "I can bear the sight of a peasant woman without disgust. That piece of simple cloth that covers her head, the hair that sparsely falls across her cheeks, those tattered rags that half cover her, that poor short petticoat that doesn't cover half her legs, her naked feet covered

> with muck cannot wound me. It is the image of a state I respect; its the ensemble of the lack of grace of a necessary and unfortunate condition for which I have pity."

After he got his new robe, his view changed drastically. It became a part of his identity. This led him to believe that every other object in his home must reflect his worth, and so he went on a spending spree that buried him in debt. And so he wrote:

> "The poor man may take his ease without thinking of appearances, but the rich man is always under a strain."

So how did a robe cause Diderot so much pain?

What We Really Want

Diderot was actually correct about how material possessions are intertwined with our identity. The richer we become, the more things become a way of expressing ourselves.

Clothes that we wear no longer only cover our skin, but also reflect our social standing and taste.

Geoffrey Miller who is an evolutionary psychologist wrote a book titled "Spent" the following about one of the main reasons why we buy things:

> "Humans evolved in small social groups in which image and status were all-important, not only for survival, but for attracting mates, impressing friends, and rearing children. Today we ornament ourselves with goods and services more to make an impression on other people's minds than to enjoy owning a chunk of matter — a fact that renders 'materialism' a profoundly misleading term for much of consumption. Many products are signals first and material objects second. Our vast social-primate brains evolved

to pursue one central social goal: to look good in the eyes of others."

It is ironic that we continue to buy more and more things to signal virtue. The reality is that the pursuit of status is actually something that only individuals with low-status do. Only those with low self-worth would care about how others perceive them, so they tend to chase after someone's approval. This is why we chase after possessions.

This also explains why large corporations sunk a lot of money into establishing their branding. Take the iPhone and BMW, for example. They advertise to everyone regardless of their income level. Their main goal is not to sell you their product, not directly anyway. They want you to believe in the identity and value of their products. It is not just an object, but a status symbol. Only a few can afford this luxury, and so people flock to buy those products, believing that these items signal their status.

The Pursuit of Status

It is funny when you think about it. Many of us are unhappy about our own situation, and yet we have never been richer throughout history. The problem is in the nature of the game.

By definition, status is hierarchical. Both in the animal kingdom and ours, there can only be one top dog who can get the best out of everything. This means, to climb up the social hierarchy, someone has to go down. This makes the pursuit of status a zero-sum game. Your gain is someone's loss. If we want to have more than our neighbor, we will never have enough. This is not a game with an end. If you want to move up to the top, you need to push everyone else down. This is an impossible task. All you can do here is just maintain your position. So, what do we do?

You may think that the best thing to do is to forego this game altogether.

Unfortunately, this may not work out for you. Social hierarchy is a deeply-rooted concept in history and it is critical to our ancestors. It helped determine who got the first choice of mate and meat. Our ancestors purposefully did this so that the most important people in the group continued to protect and guide them. Those people bore the responsibility of protecting others, in return for the privilege they enjoyed. While we no longer need such protection, status still serves the same purpose. In this regard, we have not evolved much at all.

Thankfully, the game of status does not have to be played this way. Even though we are biologically inclined to chase status, it does not mean that you have to buy more things. A larger house may mean that you have to spend more than half of your life working. The same can be applied to everything else with varying degrees.

Everything costs time and money to acquire, but they often do not have that much intrinsic value. Instead, why don't we pursue other activities that still signal at our value, but also have an inherent value? Here are some ideas:

- Work out at the gym: One of the main reasons people work out at the gym is so they can look better and they can tell others about it. In addition to having a fit body that you can be proud of, you also have the added benefit of being healthy.
- Teaching or helping others: They say that the best way to make yourself happy is by helping others. When you help other people learn something, it is a demonstration of expertise. You show them your status as an expert in that subject matter, at least relatively. This is also a great opportunity for you to hone your skills and refine your own understanding.

Jim Rohn once said that the best reward in becoming a millionaire is not the money that you make, but rather the kind of person you have to be in order to become one.

To sum it up, it is really easy for us to get lost chasing after more and more things without stopping to consider what we really want. This is the danger of mindless consumption. Most of the time, all we get are the substitutes or replicas of what we really desire. It will take time, effort, honesty, and reflection to figure out what we want in life.

So, before you embark on your next pursuit for status, stop and take some time to think. From what Diderot has taught us, it can be very costly if you chase the wrong thing.

Forego Ego and Vanity

"Throw out your conceited opinions, for it is impossible for a person to begin to learn what he thinks he already knows." – Epictetus

Epictetus faced some challenges as a teacher because his students said that they wanted to be taught, but believed that they knew everything deep down. If you are a teacher and lecturer, perhaps you know about this all too well. It is all about ego and arrogance. We think that we have learned enough and are better than other people in the room.

This kind of thinking is dangerous, even more so today.

The information we have today is not enough to solve problems in the future, not to mention that it can be an obstacle for sharper thinking. We live in an age where a bad decision can literally ruin your entire life. Even in ancient times, Marcus Aurelius said that the universe is changing, and life is just an opinion.

You can think of this as a positive feedback loop, in which the result amplifies the cause, which then amplifies the result and so on. When you are well-versed in any field, you know exactly where you are lacking. You may be good at math, but literature is way outside your comfort zone. Those who are ignorant do not know where they are lacking, so they assume that they know everything. This prevents them from learning anything new, which continues the vicious cycle. In any problem-solving process, the first thing you must do is acknowledge that the problem is real. The same applies to personal growth. You need to recognize that you can improve upon yourself before you can start improving your inner qualities.

That is why many brilliant minds today spend a lot of time learning by various means. They know that there is always something new they can learn.

On the Importance of Staying a Student

It is natural for us to become and remain complacent.

After taking our time going through school and college to acquire the knowledge and skills necessary, we believe that we do not need to grow further. We feel justified in resting because we develop a sense of competence and accomplishment. We believe that we have arrived at our destination, even though this is only a rest stop.

This is a very dangerous mindset to have nowadays. We often never have enough information to make decisions to solve tomorrow's problems. The lack of information proves to be obstacles for future development since our fixed paradigms stop us from developing new perspectives.

We would not have developed as a race as we have today if we did not have an evolution on our side. Everything evolves and develops based on the circumstances around it. Humans are the same way, too. To prevent us from making bad decisions or being lost in the ever-changing societies, we need to keep evolving.

How do we keep up with the changes? Complacency is another form of procrastination we talked about. It prevents us from learning new things. We do not know how we have stagnated until it is too late to change.

It seems to be an arduous task to keep working on ourselves for our whole life. There is one person we can learn from, and that person is Frank Shamrock.

Frank Shamrock

First, let us take a look at mixed martial arts. It is one of the most popular and fastest evolving sports. It uses the best and most effective techniques from every single fighting style. If you want to be successful in this sport, you need to learn how to adapt and respond to recent developments.

Frank Shamrock understands that very well. He holds his place as a reigning champion throughout his career. He manages to stay on top of everyone. Considering how fierce the competition is in this field, it is incredible how he maintains his position.

He achieved this feat by becoming a student of the game. Shamrock uses a system called "Plus, Minus, and Equals." Ryan Holiday explained in a book titled "Ego Is the Enemy" that Shamrock believed that a fighter needs someone better to learn from if they want to become better. A fighter also needs someone weaker or lesser than them that they can teach, and also another person that is equal to them that they can challenge themselves against.

By having these three individuals, Shamrock is able to get real and constant feedback about what he knows and doesn't know, from every perspective. It helps keep him grounded, preventing him from developing an ego. Frank Shamrock said, "false ideas about yourself destroy you." So, let us break down his system.

Plus: Have Someone to Learn From

"If you cannot see where you are going, ask someone who has been there before." – J. Loren Norris

The only thing preventing us from growing is the belief that we no longer need to grow. Thinking that we know everything that we need to is lethal to our professional and personal life. This is something that some college students think after graduation. They believe that a paper tied up in a fancy red ribbon is going to get then a six-digit income. We all know how well that works for them. Spending more than twenty years in schools and college is not going to be enough. We need to learn much more than that.

Having a mentor or coach who is experienced in the field will be immensely useful as they can prevent us from falling into that kind of thinking. It puts your ego down because the student knows very well that they are not better than the master he is under.

Take a look at Alexander the Great. He had Aristotle as a tutor, from whom he learned governance and ethics before he went on to establish his empire. Helen Keller had Anna Sullivan as her tutor, who taught her how to read and write. Michael Jordan had Phil Jackson and Dean Smith to help him win.

No matter who you are, no matter what your talent and abilities are, there is always someone out there who can help you improve. They see the potential inside us as well as the mistakes we have.

The best thing is that there are mentors everywhere. We live in an age where information is accessible and at the tip of our fingers. Courses, books, and podcasts online contain the knowledge and wisdom of great minds throughout the ages. If you look hard enough, you will certainly find someone to learn from. As they say, "when the student is ready, the teacher will appear."

Minus: Have Someone to Teach

"No one learns as much about a subject as one who is forced to teach it." – Peter Drucker

It goes without saying that you cannot teach without learning. Otherwise, you'd be a bad teacher.

The phenomenon in which we learn through teaching is called the protégé effect. You can actually learn more by teaching than by learning alone. This has been proven in many studics that found students can recall information more accurately and apply it more effectively if they tutored others.

It actually makes a lot of sense. You need to consolidate your knowledge and think about the topic from multiple angles before you can teach someone about the subject matter. You always learn something new about it when you need to deconstruct a topic and reformulate it so others can understand.

"If you can't explain it simply, you don't understand it well enough." – Albert Einstein

Jim Rohn also said that you are the average of the five people you spend the most time with. This points out the fact that you do not need to worry about finding and being with people who are better than you. Learning opportunities are everywhere.

Equal: Have Someone to Challenge

"The healthiest competition occurs when average people win by putting above average effort." – Colin Powell

If you have been following sports, you know that some of the greatest achievements are made at the highest level of competition.

Competition pushes us to our limits. It fuels our primal, Darwinian instinct that only the best shall live. It creates a do-or-die mentality that is very useful for us in certain situations. Moreover, you and your competitors can learn a lot from each other. In many cases,most people are not afraid to exchange some tricks and ideas with one another. A fair, healthy competition breeds mutual respect, which creates a starting point for future collaboration.

Therefore, it is essential that you find your scene where you can compete. Ernest Hemingway moved to Paris in the 1920s so that he could join a scene of expatriate writers and artists who lived in the Left Bank. He found his scene where his peers were. Without relocating to Paris, he would never have developed the skills and connections he needed to become a successful writer.

All of the greatest human achievements are not done singlehandedly. You will need someone who can motivate you to push yourself forward in the face of uncertainty and difficulty.

Always Remain a Student

We are living in an age where everyone thinks that they know enough. In many ways, we are opinionated rather than informed. For some of us, we stopped learning after school. We ignore the latest developments and will shut everything out, preventing us from learning anything new. It's worth repeating what Epictetus said:

"It is impossible to learn that which one thinks he already knows."

It is alright if you do not know everything. Nobody does. Shamrock's entire career was built on this fact alone. This was his competitive advantage because he understood where he lags behind, and the work he needs to do to fix those problems. Even though he was, in our eyes, on top of the world, he remained a student and kept learning.

We should try to do the same as well.

Stand Your Ground

"In doing nothing men learn to do evil."
– Cato

Throughout his career that was based mainly on compromise, Cato was very stubborn in his beliefs. He was steadfast in a sense that he believed that there were no shades of grey. All vices are the same, and so are the virtues.

You would be right if you think that this is a very high standard. It is true that many things can only be accomplished through compromise. However, we are willing to compromise far from what we should. We forgo our principles just to be tolerated or to gain monetary benefits.

Cato with his ridiculous standards upset both his political allies and opponents because he was immovable. Compromise was not an option for him. He demanded that his family and friends adopt his stance, with no room for flexibility. Adhering to this high standard did not make him the most likable person, but it did give him unshakable authority. Nothing could move his conscience, so he became Rome's moral arbiter of right and wrong.

Of course, you do not need to be like him. You need to stand your ground because if you stand for nothing, you will fall to everything.

Chapter 5: On Mindfulness Practices

Mental tranquility, or mindfulness, is not easy to accomplish. Being able to be aware of one's own mind and body during stressful situations is essential for Stoics. Developing this takes time and effort, but how does mindfulness relate to Stoicism?

Stoic Mindfulness

> "What thing, out of all those that go to make up our lives, is done better by those who are inattentive? [...] Do you not realize that when once you let your mind go wandering, it is no longer within your power to recall it?" – Epictetus

Ancient Stoics trained themselves to develop a special form of on-going self-awareness, which we describe as "mindfulness," although it is somewhat different from Buddhist meditation practice. Ancient Stoics said that we should always be mindful, living in the moment, and always be aware of the character of our thoughts and actions. This form of mindfulness is called "Prosochê." A French scholar Pierre Hadot extensively documented in the book titled "Philosophy as a Way of Life" of how psychological exercises can be found in the literature of ancient philosophy, especially Stoicism.

"Attention (prosochê) is the fundamental Stoic spiritual attitude. It is a continuous vigilance and presence of mind, self-consciousness which never sleeps, and a constant tension of the spirit. Thanks to this attitude, the philosopher is fully aware of what he does at each instant, and he wills his action fully." – Hadot

To the Stoics, achieving mindfulness through breathing does not make it a helpful exercise, although there are ways to modify it to make it so. It is not about giving the mind a brief break from the daily hectic of life, but rather to focus on our judgments, especially our value judgments and whether we place value on things outside our control. You may not even need to force yourself to change as it can occur just by observance alone. However, meditation also allows you to take a step back from your own train of thoughts and actions, and observe how they carry you mindlessly along, and you can choose to not waste time on them. In many cases, less is more. Quick mindfulness meditation as simple as breathing or meditating can help you save time and energy throughout your day. By toning down the frequency and duration of unnecessary activities and simplifying your life, you can achieve mental tranquility. This should be the first step because you need to sort out your thought process first before you can move on to adapting yourself to other Stoic practices. It starts with self-observation and noticing what you are actually doing from moment to moment, as you are doing it. From there, you can try out meditating.

Meditation

Meditation has been proven to be the best way to achieve mental tranquility and is practiced widely throughout history in many religions. The entire process is very simple and it should not take you too much time to prepare everything. If you want to reap lasting benefits of meditation, however, you need to dedicate or find a permanent place where you will spend your time meditating. Here, you will learn all the general ideas of a good meditation practice that you can use to get started right away.

What You Will Need

Although there are several products out there that claim to help you achieve a more mindful or wholesome meditation, you do not need them to successfully reap the benefits of meditation. Here are three main things to get you started:

A Place to Meditate

Quite obvious, but meditation veterans will tell you that the location is crucial. You need to find a place with enough light (but not too much), open enough to let the fresh air come through, and with enough space, for you to be able to open up. It is worth mentioning that the place should help you feel relaxed even before you begin, so the decoration or the color of the room should also reflect that. One more thing to consider is noise. It should be kept at a minimum level so you will not get distracted.

A Seat

While there are standing and walking types of meditation, sitting meditation is the most practiced type of meditation and here is where you should start. You need something to rest your body on, but not to the point that you fall asleep. You need to be aware of your body, while still being relaxed. So, sitting is ideal for you. Here, you have a few alternatives:

- **A Chair:** If you are starting out with meditation, or you have back problems, or you find meditation cushions to be uncomfortable, you can use a chair. In fact, you should start off by sitting on a chair first as it helps you to keep your back straight in a sitting position. Keeping your position upright is crucial in any meditation, and the backrest of the chair will help you with that. Of course, once you become more familiar and comfortable with meditation, it may be worth switching to a meditation cushion.

- **A Meditation Cushion:** A meditation cushion is the most common thing that people sit on when they meditate. It is so popular because of the fact that it is the easiest to sit on with an upright position. That, in turn, helps you stay alert and keep the quality of the meditation high. Of course, a meditation cushion does not have a backrest, but when you slump against it, you will lose focus. The meditation cushion forces you to keep your back straight, and maintaining that healthy form as well as keeping you focused on yourself.

- **A Meditation Bench:** If you are tall, have leg problems, or that meditation cushion is just too uncomfortable and counterproductive to your meditation, you might want to give the meditation bench a shot. Just like the meditation cushion, you still need to sit upright without the backrest so you will not have the urge to slump. What makes this different from the meditation cushion is that it absorbs more weight than the cushion, so it takes off the pressure from your legs and makes meditation comfortable for you.

Timer

A timer is another crucial tool to help you meditate. When you close your eyes and go on a journey of self-discovery that is meditation, it is easy to lose track of time. Having a timer does come in handy, and it is built into most phones. There is really no need for you to buy a physical meditation timer when your phone works just as well. All that you really need from the timer is to tell you when you should stop meditating so you don't have to break away from the trance just to look at the time.

What to Do

Here is where many beginners stumble. It is not because it is hard to meditate, it is just that they do not know what to do. Many meditation instructions out there are vague at best. Here, we will focus on the two things you need to do:

How to Sit

You may see different forms of meditation in many places such as in movies or television, or even on posters. With little information given, beginners may be unsure about the proper way to sit down and meditate. It all boils down to personal preference, which is why you see so many different forms. Still, they share some common traits that you should know:

- **The Eyes:** The goal of meditation is to make you focus on yourself. Some types of meditation may say that you need to close your eyes. Others may need you to keep your eyes open. However, it really boils down to personal preference. If you can focus on your breathing better with your eyes closed, then keep them closed. Some may find that keeping their eyes closed would run the risk of them actually falling asleep. You can avoid this by opening your eyes slightly and focusing on a single space in front of you. Again, if this becomes distracting, then keep your eyes closed and try to remain alert.

- **The Head:** When you meditate, look slightly upward. This form opens your body up and helps the body relax. It also takes off some pressure from your neck when you lean your head back a bit. If you have a bad neck posture (slump forward), then this posture can also help you.

- **The Hands:** Again, you will undoubtedly see different positions. Again, you just need to put them wherever they feel most comfortable for you. Some like to intertwine their fingers, some like to put one palm above the others, and some just put them on the leg. Find out whichever works best for you and stick to it.

- **The Back:** The most important thing to keep in mind is that you need to keep your back straight and erect. If you sit on a chair, it is best not to rest against it. Keep an upright posture so you can concentrate easier.

- **The Legs:** Just like your hands, cross them in whatever way that feels the most comfortable to you. Some prefer putting them in a pretzel-like position (or lotus position), but if it becomes uncomfortable for you, just cross them like you normally do.

What's next?

The one thing that you need to control (and might be the most difficult thing to control) is your attention. In your life, your attention may be scattered to many things at once. Your phone, the conversation, the time, work, and many other things. Meditation challenges you to gather all of your focus and put it all in a single place: your breathing.

Sounds easy enough, right? Probably. Now that you have everything ready, you can start meditating on the following steps.

- **Get Comfortable:** Go to your meditation place, get the timer ready, and don't forget your chair or meditation cushion or meditation bench. It might help you focus if you dim the lights a bit, or just shut them all off so you can focus better.

- **Set Your Timer:** If you are just starting out, then you should go for 5 minutes of meditation. Some go for 10 minutes or even 30 minutes. We recommend that you to start small first. If you are unfamiliar with meditation, you will find that keeping your attention on your breathing for 5 minutes can be difficult.

- **Focus:** Start the timer, and close your eyes and your mouth. Focus on your breathing as it comes in and out. Here, you can focus on any aspects of your breathing. Whatever works best for you, of course. Some focus on how the air enters and exits the nose. Some focus on how it inflates and deflates the lungs. Some focus on the stomach. You can even focus on the sound you make when you breathe. Pacing is also important. Keep it slow and steady. Take slow and deep breaths. Observe the way you breathe, but try your very best to keep your mind empty. This leads to our third step.

- **Keep Your Mind Empty:** Try your best to not think of anything. Focus all of your attention and mind on the breath that you are taking. It is easy to get distracted. Do not worry about how well you do your meditation. Just focus on doing it.If you do get distracted and your mind wanders, do your best to gently guide it back to your breaths. It can be just as easy to become frustrated when your mind wanders constantly, especially if you are just starting out. You tend to lose focus when you exhale because that is more subtle than when you inhale and it can be hard to concentrate on. If you find it hard to concentrate, try counting your breath when you exhale. That way, you can concentrate on your breath when you breathe in, and concentrate on the number when you breathe out. We recommend you count up to 5 and then reset to 0.

Some Additional Tips

There are also a few more things you need to keep in mind when you meditate so you can reap all the benefits of meditation:

1. **Try to do it first thing in the morning, and before bed:** Not only will you not forget to do it on a daily basis, meditation also serves as the transition from a relaxed state of the body after a restful sleep to the more active state when you get on with your daily life. You can skip the step entirely and launch yourself into the day full of stressful events, but your body may not catch on and you will feel tired. It will also be hard for you to focus when you

work. Meditation is a great bedtime routine as well.

2. **Develop a loving attitude:** When you meditate, many things (good and bad) will come up in your mind. Look at them as if they are there to help you. A way to develop positive thinking is by seeing everything in a kind, and loving way.

3. **Don't worry too much about how you're doing it:** Some people become frustrated or worried that they did not meditate properly when they get distracted for a few seconds during their session. The thing is, there is no way you can meditate perfectly. There will be flaws and you will get distracted sometimes. When your mind wanders, gently guide it back to your breathing. You will get better at this as time passes.

4. **Don't ignore whatever comes:** Meditation is also a journey of self-discovery. When you meditate, most of the small and insignificant things will vanish. However, some deeper, more pressing issues tend to arise. These issues are most likely the source of your

anger, anxiety, or frustration. You will recognize them as they come. Although you should just brush it aside when you meditate, it is worth staying with them for a moment. It can be tricky to stay with those thoughts without feeling the negativity, but it can help you pinpoint the source of your sorrow so you can address them later.

5. **Befriend yourself:** As mentioned earlier, meditation is more than just about relaxing. It is also a journey of self-discovery. When you meditate, be aware of your own thoughts. Chances are they are responsible for your behavior. However, observe yourself in a friendly way, and do not criticize yourself too badly. Give yourself some love and try to understand yourself.

6. **Commit:** This is where most beginners fail. They try it once or twice, and then give up and say that meditation does not help them at all. In reality, it does. All it takes is some effort. Develop a habit of meditation on a daily basis, and you will soon notice the difference.

7. **Comfort and alertness:** We talked about this before, but this needs to be stressed again. No matter what type or form of meditation you practice, comfort and alertness should always be a high priority. If you are uncomfortable, it will be hard for you to concentrate. If you are too comfortable, you run the risk of snoozing off. Find that perfect balance where you are comfortable but alert at the same time. In the end, the pose, form, or placements of hands and legs are up to you. You choose which one is the best for you, and stick to it.

8. **Focus:** If you find it hard to focus on your breathing, or want to try something a little bit more difficult and different, then there are other alternatives that you could try out. You can try to focus on a certain part of the body at a time. Be aware of how that body part feels. You can even try to work your way up from your feet up to your head during meditation. Alternatively, you can place your attention on the light in the room. You can even switch up your point of focus on a daily basis. One day, you focus on

the sounds, and the next day, you can focus on the light.

9. **When you're done, smile:** Meditation is also the process of giving yourself the attention you need and deserve. In order to develop positive thinking, smile after you have finished your meditation. Be thankful that you allow yourself some quality time to meditate. Give yourself a pat on the shoulder as if to say "Nice job" for sticking to your commitment. Everyone needs some self-love, and there is not much else to do to feed yourself just that.

Common Mistakes when Meditating

There are many ways to meditate, that much is true. Some aspects of meditation can be modified to fit your own preferences, although many people pay a little too much attention to detail. The most common mistakes people make when they are meditating is the way that they think.

- **Judging the Experience:** When you meditate, the goal is to keep you breathing steadily and your head clear. It is meant to give your head a break, the silence that it deserves. However, it is also the practice of patience and gratitude. We mentioned before how important it is to keep your mind and heart at peace when you meditate. Beginners tend to worry about whether they are doing it right, or that the meditation that they are practicing is a good one. Instead, stop worrying and focus on the fact that you are practicing meditation. Focus on yourself and the stillness of emotions.

- **Props:** There are many of them that can help you focus. However, it is also worth mentioning that you do not need them to meditate. In fact, they might even distract you from meditating. Meditation is all about inner peace, and you do not need external objects to achieve that. That does not mean that props are worthless. Try to keep them to a minimum. Keep the ones that actually keep you awake or focused.
- **Over-complications:** Nowadays, you can find hundreds of meditation techniques that have modern twists on ancient practices. While science has

contributed to these modern meditation techniques, it is worth noting that they may lack the spiritual experience. Traditional meditation techniques have been developed and have thousands of years of experience in spiritual growth, and that is what makes them a better choice for serious practitioners. Modern meditation techniques can be fun to try out, but you should stick to the traditional ones.

- **Guided Meditations:** This is a type of meditation which we will discuss later. Basically, it helps beginners and experts alike unlock the key to inner peace easier. However, it is not recommended that you use it every time when you meditate. While helpful in itself, you should learn how to access that place of silence and peace on your own. Otherwise, your own journey is not worthwhile. Of course, that does not mean that you should ditch this meditation altogether. You just need to maintain a healthy balance between guided meditations and solo meditations.
- **Spice things up** Meditation can get repetitive and boring very quickly.

When it does, you will find it hard to keep meditating. How do you avoid that? Simple. You can mix things up a bit to keep it interesting. Try meditating with your eyes open, or with soothing ambient music (if you haven't already). If you are feeling adventurous, then you can even try meditating while you are working. All you need to do is to keep your head clear and breathing deep and constant. You do not really need to sit down in a meditating position in order to start meditating. Just make sure that you are comfortable with the environment before you start.

How to Develop Awareness of Emotions and Thoughts

Your thoughts are your inner dialogue, a conversation between you and you. We have an average of six thousand thoughts a day, which we often repeat to ourselves. In many cases, these thoughts come from past experience or childhood experience. Since then, it has been repeating itself in your head. Because our cognitive abilities do not develop fully until the mid-20s, you can tell how many of these thoughts no longer serve you.

Why should we develop an awareness of our inner dialogue? After all, it seems so effortless to talk to yourself and so insignificant. By controlling how you think about yourself and what is around you, you can start to regulate and choose your own response to any event. This is key to mental tranquility.

Simply put, you want to be aware of what you are saying to yourself inside. That way, you have direct control over your choices, not your emotions. Your happiness and peace of mind depend on this. This is important because your thoughts can activate certain thought processes within you, driven purely by emotions, even painful ones. Your thoughts and the beliefs that drive them cause you to feel a certain way toward something.

Even though external events may cause you to feel or react in a certain way, they actually do not. What you feel is just a result of your mind's interpretation of reality and it tells you how to feel about it. Most of what it tells you is subconscious, coming from the beliefs that you have. These beliefs are also subconscious.

When you control what you think, not allowing your emotions to cloud your judgments, you also control your behavior. This means you can control how your life unfolds to an extent. To begin, we need to develop self-awareness to transform your thoughts.

While controlling your own emotions allows you to have a more rational approach to the situation, you also gain an understanding of the power of emotions. Learning how to use them to your advantage is just as crucial. Emotions are chemical molecules that command circuits of your body. They have a powerful influence on your beliefs, thoughts, and behaviors. Your emotions are indicators.

Just like a GPS, you can tell if you are where you want to be based on your feelings. Your success in overcoming problems depends on your ability to experience emotions and let them tell you from moment to moment as you make decisions.

For instance, when you feel good, joy, happiness, or confidence, it is a sign that your inner drives are met. However, this can be misleading because not all positive emotions mean that you are in the right place. It may work against your highest interest.

On the other hand, negative emotions are indicators that tell you that you are probably not in the right place. They make you feel stressed. Still, important events require you to put yourself through this unpleasant experience. Things such as taking an exam or dealing with an important issue help you grow, perform, and achieve some amazing things.

Therefore, it is critical that you learn how to connect empathically with unpleasant feelings like anxiety, guilt, shame, or hurt. They give you a lot more information about yourself than your positive emotions. They give you a better idea of where you are in relation to where you want to be. For instance, emotions based on fear indicate that you should stop and evaluate what other possible actions or changes that can support your visions or goals better. More often than not, the solution can be as simple as replacing a limiting belief with an energizing one. It may be more challenging because you may need to openly express your emotions to another person authentically without placing the blame on anyone.

We have seven steps to develop your awareness of your feelings and how they are connected to your thoughts.

Select a Triggering Situation to Process

First, make a list of events that trigger anger in you. Arrange them in order from the least challenging to process to the most challenging. Work on the easiest triggers, one at a time, and move gradually up to the most challenging. Take it slow because it might take you weeks. It requires patience. You need to stretch yourself outside your comfort zone but not so much that you become overwhelmed with the process. If it becomes too emotionally intense, take a break. If this happens, it's probably a good idea to get professional help from a therapist or a counselor.

Center Yourself in the Present

When you have identified and selected the trigger you wish to reflect on, take a moment and take three to five deep breaths from your diaphragm to allow yourself to relax. Focus on your breathing with your eyes closed. Notice how your body feels from the top of your head to the tip of your toes. Release any tension or tightness.

Then, imagine yourself in a safe place where you can let your guard down. Separate yourself from your emotions or thoughts by reminding yourself that you are the observer who has the creator of these emotions and thoughts. Remind yourself that this is good news as you are in control of your emotions so no one can make you feel a certain way toward something without your permission. Observe your emotions and make a mental note to yourself that anything that you feel results from past experience, from a time when you did not have the ability to know and see yourself and life from different viewpoints. Now that you are capable, you are in charge of your thought processes. You can stop this exercise whenever you want.

Identify and Feel Your Emotions and Feelings

After relaxing and preparing yourself for this reflective session, start bringing the selected trigger to mind. Remember the list we made earlier? Choose the easiest trigger and recall its most recent occurrence. Then, be aware of how that event makes you feel. Be aware of your sensations without judging. Notice how you feel inside as you take slow, deep breaths. Then, ask yourself, "What am I feeling right now?"

If you feel anger, go down another layer. Find other emotions beneath it. Anger is only a secondary emotion that protects you from feeling emotions associated with vulnerability such as fear, shame, or hurt. So, if you feel anger, ask yourself, "What underlies this anger?"

What emotions and feelings do you feel? Write them down in your philosophical journal and reflect upon them at the end or start of the day.

Feel and Notice the Location of Any Sensation in Your Body

In addition to anger, also notice how your body feels. Pause and feel each sensation as you feel each emotion. Note down what physical sensations you feel. For each motion that is triggered, ask yourself what your body feels as you imagine the triggering event. Note the location of these physical sensations. Feel that sensation and breathe deeply while placing one or both of your hands on where you feel them in your body. When you do, let go of any impulse to stop, judge, repress, or fix any of your emotions and sensations. Continue to probe them. You may notice that the sensation may be less intense over time. If you feel that anger is your primary emotion, keep asking yourself what else you feel. Try to describe that sensation and record where you feel it.

Accept Your Feelings

Dissociate yourself from your emotions by telling yourself that you are not your emotions. You are the observer and the emotions are just energy. What you feel is just pockets of energy linked to past wounds. Because you are the decision-maker in your life, you can choose to tap into this painful past through breathing and notice the energy shift, move, and release. You can choose to affirm the power that you have as the decision-maker and accept these painful feelings because it is natural to feel pain because you are human. So, calmly and confidently affirm, "I accept that I am feeling (emotion) at this moment."

Repeat this to yourself silently or aloud: "I can handle this emotion. I am strong and can handle this calmly, easily, wisely."

A great way to gain leverage on negative emotions is by remembering a time when you experienced similar emotions and handled it successfully. Because you have dealt with it once, you can do it again right now and in the future. Tell yourself, "I have handled this emotion in the past. I can do it again today, and in the future." Repeat this affirmation to yourself several times as needed until you feel a change in your emotional state and its intensity. While you are doing this, take slow deep breaths between each repetition. Remember that each time you handle this emotion, you improve your mental resilience. This will strengthen and develop your confidence and your ability to cope with negative emotions. This, in turn, allows you to learn from negative emotions and turn them into assets.

Identify What You Tell Yourself

Then, notice your thoughts as you picture the triggering event, especially any toxic thinking patterns. Your thoughts always trigger physical sensations and emotions in your body. This is just how our brain works.

Observe these thoughts from a distance, as the objective observer. Again, do not judge your experience. Use this visual. When a disturbing thought surfaces, imagine yourself sitting in a luxurious high-speed train, looking out the window, and nonchalantly observe any upsetting thoughts passing by in a flash outside the window as you sit comfortably in your seat in a safe place. Write down what you tell yourself next to the emotions and physical sensations you went through in the previous steps.

Connect Empathically

Finally, remind yourself that although other situations or people can cause painful emotions in you, they are not the cause themselves. How you interpret the situation, your self-talk, causes all of these painful emotions you feel such as guilt or frustration, resentment or anger. This is good because if how you interpret external events causes you to feel upset, you can choose to change how you interpret them and empower your confidence and ability to make the right choices.

Remember that being able to control how you interpret external events is really, really good news. That means you are in full control of your emotional responses, thoughts, and actions. You can protect your happiness and peace of mind no matter what the world throws at you. No one can make you feel a certain way toward something unless you allow it.

By understanding this, you can create statements to affirm and validate your experience, like this: "It makes sense that I feel overwhelmed because I'm telling myself that I'll never get this done, this is too much for me, or I cannot handle it."

In short, your thoughts evoke emotions inside of you, and these emotions may tell you something important that you need to know to live your life happily. These emotions may tell you how to best live your life and thrive. When you develop your awareness of these indicators (emotions and sensations), you have a better understanding of the connection between your words or thoughts to your emotions and physical sensations.

When you do, you will realize that you have a lot more control over your thoughts than you may think. You come to find out that just by making a few tweaks in the way you think, you can improve your life considerably. Changing how you experience events in a way that allows you to still remain on the life-enriching course you chose will be the best chance you will ever get in life. Your emotions, especially the painful ones, will be indicators – guides to tell you whether you are on the right path to mental tranquility. When you understand the power of shaping your emotions and how they work with your thoughts, it becomes a lot easier to confront and embrace them instead of avoiding, minimizing, or looking down on them.

In the vast and unforgiving ocean of life, your feelings act as your navigation system. Use them wisely.

Chapter 6: On Consolidation of Thoughts

"No man was ever wise by chance." – Seneca

We all have many things to do every day, but none of them entail looking into ourselves. This happens to be the most important thing for a Stoic. Through self-reflection, you are forced to question yourself and examine your assumptions of the world. This is how some have found the answers to many of the world's biggest questions.

Having a journal is one of the best ways to maintain mindfulness. Moreover, it helps boost creativity, increases gratitude, and also serves as therapy as you are your own therapist. The benefits are countless. Manyof the world's greatest minds keep a journal with them all the time so that they can record their thoughts and feelings. They are much clearer when you put them into words because you need to consult them for details and formulate phrases to express your true thoughts and feelings.

The Stoics are aware of this. The book titled "Meditations" was a personal journal of Marcus Aurelius who was one of the most powerful men in history. He took the time to record his feelings and observations, during both peace and war times.

While many people have benefited from Marcus' ideas today, it is clear that he benefited the most from his thinking and writing. His journal kept his thoughts clear and held him accountable so he continued to lead a virtuous life when anyone in his position would have become corrupt and a tyrant.

Philosophical Journal

You may already know the benefits of keeping a journal, but we want to focus on another type of journal. Instead of writing about what happened in your life, you can also take a long hard look at it from a Stoic's perspective. You can use this journal to discover your own shortcomings and then track how you have changed over time. Through constant reflection and conscious efforts put into self-improvements, you can improve your life.

So, start planning your future actions by taking into consideration the ethical framework. From there, write down what happened and see what needs to be changed. This Stoic exercise can be integrated seamlessly if you are already writing a personal journal. All you need to do is record what happened and then try to come up with how you can change based on the event.

Start by keeping a daily philosophical journal and record everyday events for at least one month. For more resources, you can refer to Marcus Aurelius' philosophical journal titled "Meditations."

Early Morning Reflection

"Cling tooth and nail to the following rule: Not to give in to adversity, never to trust prosperity, and always to take full note of fortune's habit of behaving just as she pleases, treating her as if she were actually going to do everything it is in her power to do. Whatever you have been expecting for some time comes as less of a shock." – Seneca

At the start of your day, make a habit of reflecting. It's more nuanced than you think. It's more than just planning out what you want to do during the day. It's also about priming your mind to react a certain way to the things that may happen throughout the day.

So, be thankful for the fact that you just woke up. We discussed the morbid idea of our mortality back in the first chapter, so smile and be thankful for the fact that you are alive and well. This is the first step.

Then, in addition to planning out the day ahead, plan how you want to embrace your virtues and avoid your vices. Choose a personal strength or philosophical precept that you wish to cultivate, then plan how you wish to incorporate it into the day. As always, expect to face difficulties throughout the day. So, plan ahead on how you want to respond to these events that align with your personal growth goals for the day.

Finally, remind yourself to only worry about the things you can control such as your thoughts and actions. Disregard everything else.

There are other activities you can do here. If you manage to wake up early enough and have plenty of time on your hands, you can go out for a walk and enjoy the morning sun and meditate on how you can develop yourself as a person.

While you are out walking, you can take some time to perform light exercises. You do not need a dumbbell or other fancy equipment. Just simple bodyweight exercises are enough. While you are at it, think of your own mortality and the fact that you will age.

Bedtime Reflection

In addition to reflecting in the morning and writing a journal about your day, it is a good idea to have a bedtime reflection session. So, replay the entire day mentally and then ask yourself these questions:

- Did my behavior align with my principles?
- Did I treat others in a friendly and considerate manner?
- What voices have I fought?
- Have I made myself a better person through the cultivation of my virtues?

While you are at it, feel free to plan for the next day as well. You can write down a few things you should think about in the morning in your philosophical journal. This links up seamlessly with your early morning routine and your philosophical journal.

Simply put, this activity is all about learning from your mistakes.

In your philosophical journal, you can write down one thing you want to improve the next day, no matter how insignificant it may seem. We want to focus on small but constant improvement. You may be surprised at how much you can change if you keep this up for just a month. Set a small goal and stick to it.

Other than that, remind yourself that today is finished and you can do nothing to change what happened. Accept everything that has happened, good or not.

How Journaling Leads to a Better Life

The first thing you may recall about Benjamin Franklin is the fact that he is one of the founding fathers of the United States. He helped write the famous United States Constitution and the Declaration of Independence. He defended the American Cause. However, he was more than just a politician. He was also a polymath.

Other than politics, Benjamin Franklin was known as the father of electricity. He was a scientist and inventor. He began experimenting with electricity when he accidentally shocked himself. His curiosity and fascination turned to obsession, which resulted in the invention of the lightning rod that proves useful to today.

Franklin also has his contribution to the world in the literature field. He was an essayist, newspaper publisher, and an author.

Some of his works include his own autobiography and Poor Richard's Almanac.

Although he was born into a poor family and only got two years' worth of formal education, what Franklin was able to achieve and contribute was astounding. If there ever was a self-made man, he certainly was one.

One of the things that contributed to his success was his habit of keeping a journal. Franklin had many journals throughout his entire life and used them in ways we could not imagine. While we all know the benefits and importance of keeping a journal, they were not so apparent back then. This made Franklin a different man from other men of his time. By understanding how he used his journals, we can understand what went on in his mind.

Focus

Franklin was a disciplined man. This is not surprising considering the feats he accomplished. He followed his schedule strictly. As he wrote in "The Autobiography of Benjamin Franklin":

> "The precept of Order requiring that every part of my business should have its allotted time, one page in my little book contained the following scheme of employment for the twenty-four hours of a natural day"

It sounds like your modern-day calendar, doesn't it? You're not wrong. Franklin understood that he only had 24 hours a day, and he wanted to spend them effectively. He knew how important it was to plan how he would use his time. Notably, he also tracked how he used his time and corrected it as needed. As Peter Drucker once said, "what gets measured, gets managed."

This is one of the uses Franklin had for journals. Research shows that keeping a simple to-do list is not as effective as keeping a journal. When you create a specific time for a specific activity, you are more likely to do it when the time comes. If you do not define exactly when you want to do it, you will probably not do it.

Of course, a journal has many uses. There are no specific purposes for having a journal so you can use it for productivity if you struggle to keep one. Having a journal allows you to jot down more details when you write about your activities, compared to a calendar. It is not the most obvious benefit, but it certainly helps you plan out your life.

Accountability

Franklin talked about self-improvement and lived it, making sure that he was not lying to himself. His desire to improve as a person was crucial to his success. His pursuit of excellence was all-encompassing because he sought to improve mentally, professionally, and morally. He started his moral pursuits at the early age of 20, after which he started adopting other virtuous habits.

Franklin followed thirteen virtues that he believed to be desirable. But unlike others that only preach these virtues, he lived them and tracked his progress. He wrote:

> "My intention being to acquire the habitude of all these virtues, I judg'd it would be well not to distract my attention by attempting the whole at once, but to fix it on one of them at a time; and, when I should be master of that, then to proceed to another, and so on, till I should have gone thro' the thirteen."

The thirteen virtues he tried to acquire were carefully thought out. At the end of each day, Franklin would evaluate himself based on these virtues and marked which virtues he violated. His goal was to keep the number of marks off his journal to a minimum. Therefore, the indicator he used to determine whether he led a life of virtue would be how pristine his journal was. These are his virtues at the age of twenty:

1. Temperance: Eat not to dullness, drink not to elevation.
2. Silence: Speak not but what may benefit others or yourself; avoid trifling conversation.
3. Order: Let all your things have their place; let each part of your business have its time.
4. Resolution: Resolve to perform what you ought; perform without fail what you resolve.
5. Frugality: Make no expense but to do good to others or yourself; i.e., waste nothing.
6. Industry: Lose no time; be always employ'd in something useful; cut off all unnecessary actions.

7. Sincerity: Use no hurtful deceit; think innocently and justly, and, if you speak, speak accordingly.
8. Justice: Wrong none by doing injuries, or omitting the benefits that are your duty.
9. Moderation: Avoid extremes; forbear resenting injuries so much as you think they deserve.
10. Cleanliness: Tolerate no uncleanliness in body, clothes, or habitation.
11. Tranquility: Be not disturbed at trifles, or at accidents common or unavoidable.
12. Chasity: Rarely use venery but for health or offspring, never to dullness, weakness, or the injury of your own or another's peace or reputation.
13. Humility: Imitate Jesus and Socrates.

You may say that these virtues set an impossibly high standard, to which you are absolutely correct. Benjamin Franklin himself did not attain his goal of perfect morality, but he did at least keep the habit of self-improvement. The journal kept him accountable and he did the best he could, which we all should strive toward. Perhaps you can incorporate these virtues into your life as well. The goal is not to follow every one of them to the letter, but rather to give you something to work toward.

Reflection

While Franklin strived not to waste an hour of his time, he always questioned the value of his work and motives behind his activities, believing that self-reflection must not be ignored.

For example, he had the habit of asking himself two questions every day when he questioned himself whether he had violated any of the thirteen virtues. At the top of his page, he wrote: "What good shall I do this day?" This allowed him to reflect the virtues he must follow and how he could improve upon his past self. At the end of the day, he wrote: "What good have I done today?"

He conducted this integrity report every day. He tracked what he did and when during his working hours, but spent some time at the end of the day asking himself why he did what he did.

He never shied away from answering difficult questions. Many of us spend our journaling hours writing inspirations and affirmations, but Franklin used his journal differently: To track his moral wrongdoings. He recorded every wrongdoing he had committed on the left side of his journal, and what he had done to right the wrong on the right.

Among his moral shortcomings was his tolerance of slavery. He allowed for the sale of slaves to be advertised on the Pennsylvania Gazette, which he owned. He even owned slaves for himself although he was apprehensive of this practice. However, his greatest moral failing was when he agreed to a compromise that resulted in the enshrinement of slavery in the constitution.

Franklin could not right this wrong, but he did do his very best to fix his mistakes even in his elderly age. He eventually became the President of the Society for the Abolition of Slavery, and actively and publicly spoke out against such practice.

Journaling

Franklin certainly would not have been the person he was without his journals. After studying his life, we can see how keeping a journal gives you a better sense of control over ourselves.

Many of us focus more on how forward-thinking journaling can be. That is certainly alright, but it may not translate into the results we seek. One of the problems with journaling is that we get a sense of accomplishment from writing things down, but that is only therapeutic. It does not mean that we will take action to get the results we desire.

As we mentioned earlier, Franklin did not use the journal to inspire himself. He used it to hold himself accountable for his wrongdoings. His journal compels him to take action – to do the right thing and become a better person. Franklin knows this and took steps to improve himself instead of wishing that he would do better tomorrow.

His journaling was a keystone habit, which allows the power of journaling to manifest further than just being a mindless record of his daily life. His life was heavily based on journaling because this was a habit for him. We can learn much from Franklin's life, especially how he used his journal to learn, reflect, and account for his actions.

More importantly, you need to learn how to record your own story. It may not seem like much for you now, but small and incremental improvements can amount to much in just a month. Over the course of a lifetime, no one knows how much positive influence a journal can bring into your life.

Keystone Habits

We used the word "keystone" habit in the previous section. What exactly is it? Well, allow us to tell you a story first.

Michael Phelps is perhaps one of the most decorated Olympians of all time. He has won 28 medals in many swimming categories and is the current champion of many world records even though he has now retired. His 80-inch wingspan and flexible ankles made him a better swimmer than a runner. He was a gifted swimmer, but that was not the entire story.

What was not so well-known about his success was the fact that his life has been built on a few habits. They were instilled into him to turn him into a world-class swimmer. Bob Bowman, his swimming coach, knew that Phelps had the potential to be a great swimmer, but for him to become world-class, he needed habits to turn him into the best mental swimmer there was.

Then the 2008 Olympics came about and Bowman was proven correct. Phelps went on to win eight medals in a single Olympics, making him the first person to have ever accomplished such a feat. When Bowman was asked about how Phelps prepared for the Olympics (possibly suspecting that he had a different training regiment, diet plans, etc.) Bowman said:

"If you ask Michael what was going on inside his head before the competition, he would say that he wasn't really thinking about anything. He was just following the program. But that's not the entire story. It's more like his habits have taken over. Everything went according to plan. The warm-up laps were just like he visualized. The stretches went as he planned. His headphones are playing exactly what he expected."

What many of us see as tedious, Bowman saw as essential and indispensable. He then went on to explain that the actual race was just another event in a set of patterns that started earlier that day. The pattern pointed Phelps to nothing but victory, so of course, winning is just a natural extension.

The Power of Keystone Habits

Habits automate your actions and outcomes, making everything predictable. When our body is on autopilot, we can perform as expected no matter what the environment you are put in is. That matters if every single action counts, especially if you are competing at the highest level like Phelps.

Phelps had many habits incorporated into his routines. He would visualize his perfect race, with each stroke, turn and finish done in perfection, before and after going to bed. His stretching regimen follows a certain pattern, starting with his arms and ending at his ankles. He knows how long his warm-up will take before each race.

Now, it sounds like you need to pick up a lot of habits in order to achieve something amazing. It is not. You see, these habits were not developed one by one. Some habits compound, meaning that they go together. So, if you take up one habit, a few more will follow naturally.

In the book called "The Power of Habit," Charles Duhigg called these habits the keystone habits. Unlike ordinary habits, keystone habits create positive effects that go over into other areas by starting a chain reaction that shifts many other patterns. This transforms everything over time. Think of a keystone habit as a switch that you just flip to cause this chain reaction.

What A Keystone Habit Looks Like

A keystone is characterized by its ability to trigger a set of behaviors.

For example: Suppose that you start to track your food to know how many calories you were consuming. Eventually, after seeing the numbers, you start exercising, then reducing your carbohydrates intake. That means that you started to order takeouts less frequently, and started cooking for yourself more and more.

You may pick up all of these habits without realizing it. You may look back one day and be surprised at how such a trivial act of keeping track of your food motivated you to lead a much healthier lifestyle. If you were to take a closer look, you may realize that the process was actually simple.

You become more aware of what you are eating and how many calories you are consuming. After assessing your eating habits, you start going for runs and going to the gym. Then, you think that it makes sense to further complement your efforts by optimizing your diet and starting to eat healthier food. Based on where you live, you may start to learn how to cook your own meals to follow through with your new lifestyle.

So, what we have was a small act of curiosity that led to a series of habits that make you lead a healthier life. A small change can have a drastic effect on your life. For Franklin, his keystone habit of journaling led him down a virtuous life. You can too.

Building Your Keystone Habit

You have many options to establish a keystone habit. In reality, it does not matter which action you choose because it does not cause a chain reaction. It is the intent behind the act. As Duhigg writes:

> "The power of a keystone habit draws from its ability to change your self-

image. Basically, anything can become a keystone habit if it has this power to make you see yourself in a different way."

So, the range of habits is unlimited. Even actions that do not seem connected can yield unexpected benefits. Here are some keystone habits you should pick up:

- Wake up early: If you can, try to sleep earlier so you can get up early. That way, you have an hour or two to yourself which you can use to pursue your hobbies or other activities you are interested in. This can allow you to spend more time reading or working on your passion project. This extra time gives you an edge over your competitors by allowing you to master difficult skills, increasing your sense of possibility and confidence.
- Make your bed: It sounds silly, true, but this simple action can give you a better

sense of control. When you tidy up your room, the first thing you should do is tidy the bed, so everything looks easier. Plus, doing this in the morning gives you a little boost in discipline and confidence, allowing you to go on to accomplish other things during the day. This is something that Admiral William McRaven had to do when he was a Navy SEAL. It was his keystone habit. You can find out more in his book "Make Your Bed."

- Meditate: We feel that this is worth mentioning again. There are many benefits associated with meditation, including improved self-awareness, reduction of anxiety, and greater emotional stability. The mental tranquility this brings can help you in decision-making.

So, let us not confine ourselves to specific behaviors. Start getting your life sorted, make your bed, get up early if you can, and you will start seeing the difference. The point is: start doing something that you will eventually enjoy and work from there.

Chapter 7: Overcoming Negative Emotions

In this chapter, we will discuss how you can deal with negative emotions in the Stoic way.

Stay Focused

"If a person doesn't know to which port they sail, no wind is favorable." – Seneca

Thanks to modern-day capitalism, we are spoiled for choice. Whether it is food, entertainment, or travel, we have many more options than what people used to a few decades ago. Still, this does not benefit us. When we have so many alternatives, we become stunned by indecision.

This phenomenon is known as the paradox of choice. It is the overload of information when our brain is presented with so much data. Our brain cannot keep up with the amount. When that happens, we often choose to maintain the status quo.

This is one of the main problems we face every day. With so many things to choose from, we do not fully commit to a particular path. We either do everything at once or put off making decisions altogether. This often results in us never really making much progress anywhere.

In this regard, the Stoics focused on purposeful actions. We need to ensure that we do not take action just as a reaction to our circumstances. We need to make sure that our actions have an intention, a purpose.

Develop an Internal Locus of Control

"Man is disturbed not by things, but by the views he takes of them." – Epictctus

To start things off, you need to know what you can and cannot control. Many things that happen in our lives are outside our realm of control. The stoics know this undeniable truth and instead focus on what they can do to better the situation.

Epictetus was born a slave so it would seem that he had no reason to believe that he had control over anything. Cursed with a broken leg by his master, anyone would guess that he would live and die in poverty.

Anyone would fall into despair in such a situation, but not Epictetus. He saw things differently. Even though his property and even his body were not within his realm of control, he understood that his opinions, desires, and aversions still belonged to him. These were the few things he owned, and he made peace with that.

What about us? We take so many things for granted that we become frustrated very easily. We are so used to the comfort of our own home and technology that even a minor inconvenience can make our face turn red with rage. If the internet chokes for a second, or the traffic is only a minute slower, we would be annoyed if not outright angry.

What causes us to be this angry? From what Epictetus said, it is not the breakdowns or dysfunctions that upset us. This unhappiness stems from choice. We choose to feel angry at these minor inconveniences. We have no one but ourselves to blame for the way we respond to external events that affect our internal state of mind.

Basically, we have the power to be happy no matter what goes on in our lives. It is not the external events that cause us to be unhappy. It is how we feel toward them.

Guard Your Time

We're tight-fisted with property and money, yet think too little of wasting time, the one thing about which we all should be the toughest misers." – Seneca

Time is a commodity we all spend, and it is a priceless one at that. Unlike other assets, no amount of money can buy us another second of time. Once lost, you cannot regain it. The Stoics understood that well. So, learn how to make the most out of what little time you have.

Those who carelessly throw away their time on insignificant entertainment just for pure pleasure will find themselves at the end of the road with nothing to show for it. Procrastination is dangerous, hence the reason sloth is one of the seven deadly sins. What you put off until tomorrow will come back to bite you. Tomorrow is not always guaranteed, so if you can do it today, do it.

But being resourceful with your time is much more than that. Some people may find themselves giving their time away freely to others. This is just as bad as wasting time. Many of us allow people and other obligations to take up our time too easily. We make promises without giving much thought to what they entail. Calendars and schedules should be used to help us plan our time effectively, not to enslave us.

The effect of procrastination is restricted when you have a deadline. You know you can put things off until tomorrow, and then rush to complete the work just the night before the deadline. We have all made this same mistake which is not so bad because it works out in the end, sort of. There is another problem, though. We stop procrastinating when we are met with a deadline. What if the deadline is not there? There is one for the assignment or project. But what of other things such as visiting your family, taking care of your health, exercising, working on your relationship, or working on yourself? They don't have deadlines, do they? This is where procrastinating becomes very deadly. The deadline is not there, so we do not feel as compelled to do something, but then we would regret not doing it until it is too late.

Regardless of which category you fall into, know that time is limited. We tend to think that we have plenty of time. We actually don't. Let us put this into perspective.

In the United States, the average lifespan of a person is 27,375 days. If you are 25, then you have 18,250 days to live. If you are 50, you have roughly 9,125 days, and if you are 65, 3,650 days. As you can see, we do not have much time in our lives. To make matters worse, suppose that you sleep for eight hours a day. That is already a third of your time spent just on sleeping alone. Do you have an 8-hour job? That's another third. We have roughly 34% of our time to waste on other things such as watching TV, listening to music, and basically procrastinating. Are you willing to risk what little time you have on these things? Make every second count.

On Sorting Out Your Priorities

We all strive to do more in our lives. We get out there, chase after our goals and dreams, and make connections. Only when we have those can we make our mark in this world. However, you will tire eventually. After all, we can do anything but not everything. We can only do so much. There are only 24 hours a day, so there is only so much we can do no matter how productive or effective we are.

To make matters worse, our decision-making is lacking compared to the abundance of information and choices available. We pursue all the opportunities we see without stopping to think carefully. We decide not to decide carefully. There is nothing wrong pursuing opportunities, but you will reach a saturation point eventually. You will reach a point where there are so many responsibilities you need to fulfill that you cannot commit to a better role or fulfill your obligations. By then, you will be burned out and it's too late.

It appears that there is a better way to go about managing your time. We all know this, and yet we keep wasting our time on trivial matters. Why is that?

Hell Yeah Or No

Derek Sivers wasn't planning on establishing a large business when he started CD Baby. He just wanted to sell his CDs online, but he became a successful independent musician. When he could not find anyone to help him, he went out on his own and built an online store from scratch. It worked out for him very well because he never stopped chasing down opportunities and putting himself out there.

However, somewhere down the road, he, Derek realized something.

He realized that he was not always happy about networking or attending conferences. These things led him to develop a habit of agreeing to do more and more out of obligation, which took away his valuable time and money. He had set himself up to make default choices that were not always the best for him.

From that point on, he created a new philosophy to guide his decisions, especially when he was about to make a commitment. This was to prevent him from overcommitting. It the philosophy goes like this:

> "If you're not saying "HELL YEAH!" about something, say "no." When you say no to most things, you leave room in your life to really throw yourself completely into that rare thing that makes you say "HELL YEAH!"

This may not make sense to those who do not make the most of their time, though. If you fall into this category, then by all means, put yourself out there and pursue opportunities. However, this is often not the case for many of us. We have opportunities that we are capitalizing on, but we always want more.

Derek said in his book "Anything You Want," that we only have a limited amount of time every day. So, we all should strive to make the most out of it while we still have enough room to capitalize on better opportunities. Only work on the things that are meaningful and that you care about. Saying yes to less is the way to go.

The 90% Rule

Time is the most valuable commodity and trade-offs are often needed when you are at full capacity. Your entire life boils down to a series of transactions – time and money for something else. Everything you do has an opportunity cost and it may be more costly than not doing anything.

Therefore, we all need an essentialist approach to life. It is prioritizing your tasks based on the time you have, and knowing that we need to practice self-selection to really thrive.

Greg McKeown also advocates for this in the book called "Essentialism." He said that only when you allow yourself to stop trying to do everything, to stop saying yes, can you make the highest contribution to things that really matter.

McKeown gives his 90 percent rule: Every opportunity should be scrutinized under extreme criteria. We should pursue opportunities that are rated at 9 on the scale from 1 to 10. No matter how good the 7s and 8s are, we should pass that up unless we are absolutely sure that we have more time to spare for the 9s and 10s. Remember those good opportunities are different from the right ones.

McKeown knows that there are many trivial opportunities that may be good, but not as important or meaningful. There are only a few that mean the most to him. Again, we only have so much time, so we should pursue opportunities that help us to reach where we want to go. Therefore, it is essential that you only commit to the vital few commitments that are important to you.

Fear of Missing Out

Of course, we cannot accurately assess whether the opportunity is just good, or important to us.

When we talk about living a better life, we tend to talk about adding more things rather than simplifying and removing things from our lives. As we become more and more interconnected thanks to the Internet, we are more easily influenced by each other as well. If a friend of yours does something, you feel compelled to join in because we would feel excluded and anxious otherwise.

There is actually a name for this: FOMO (fear of missing out), aka peer pressure.

This fear is everywhere, and you probably have experienced it yourself in middle or high school. It is the fear that you may be missing out on an opportunity or the fear that you did not meet someone you should or the fear that you are lagging behind. We struggle with FOMO throughout our lives, no matter how old we are. FOMO is also one of the reasons why we overcommit.

Here, McKeown proposed that we should adopt the joy of missing out (JOMO). The problem with FOMO is that we think we may be missing out on something important. We just need to turn that thinking around and realize that the opportunities we are often given are not the ones that we actually need. Relish the fact that you are missing out on non-essential opportunities and place value on saying no. Know that passing on opportunities may create an opportunity as well.

We have given too much value on getting more and more when we should have been careful in what we invest in, and be happy with what little we have that actually matters.

A Question of Priorities

We tend not to have our lives straight. We often fail to prioritize the things we should really do, and if we don't somebody else will.

We prioritize different things based on our needs. We have a list of things that we consider to be priorities, and the list can be short or long. But when we prioritize everything, we prioritize nothing. As McKeown explained in Essentialism:

> "The word priority came into the English language in the 1400s. It was singular. It meant the very first or prior thing. It stayed singular for the next five hundred years. Only in the 1900s did we pluralize the term and start talking about priorities. Illogically, we reasoned that by changing the word, we could

bend reality. Somehow we would now be able to have multiple "first" things."

While having multiple priorities gives us some comfort because it shows that we have some level of ambition and makes us feel that we are making progress, in reality, it only distracts us from what is really important. When you start to internalize this truth, it gets easier for you to simplify your life and start doing less. Every time you refuse to get involved in doing something trivial, you create an opportunity for better things to come along or it gives you time to focus on working toward your goal. Trivial things are not worth our attention, so we should embrace JOMO.

On Trusting the Process

With a whopping 6 National Championships under his belt, Nick Saban, a football coach from the University of Alabama, is one of the best college football coaches the world has ever seen.

Although his names are often associated with victory, Saban does not care too much about the end result. The final scoreboard does not mean much to him. Instead, he wants his assistant coaches and players to just focus on the process. This is what he said:

> "Don't think about winning the SEC Championship. Don't think about the national championship. Think about what you need to do in this drill, on this play, at this moment. That's the process: Let's think about what we can do today, the task at hand."

This is a different perspective and it is quite refreshing. Some coaches may try to hype up their players because this is a winner-takes-all situation. You may think that it is a good idea to let your own players know what is at stake because you either win or you lose. There are no moral victories or consolidating prizes here. If you don't win, you leave empty-handed. But why does Nick Saban just focus on the process? Let us take a closer look.

You Can Only Control the Process

Sports are complex. There are many things we need to take into consideration. Many of these variables are not within the control of both the players and coaches. There are so many plays a player can make in a given situation, so many statistics, and so many countermoves that it is literally impossible for each player or coach to know or memorize. To control the entire process is pure madness.

After Nick talked to psychiatry professor Lionel Rosen, he realized that the average play players make lasts only seven seconds. So, he simplified the entire process. If it is impossible to read and execute every play to perfection for the entire match, why not just focus on those seven seconds? Maintaining perfect execution for the entire game is asking for too much, but anyone can execute a play that lasts for seven seconds with perfection. So, just execute the play, rest, and repeat. Then, you will eventually have the game.

Excellence is a step-by-step process. It requires you to excel at the first, second, third thing, and so on. The process is all about staying in the present and going through with the action that you excel in, one after another. You need to focus on executing these actions regardless of the obstacles in your way.

This was exactly what Saban's team did, and they started winning games and championships.

It's the Inner Scoreboard That Counts

If you have seen his team playing, then the sight of Saban scowling on the sidelines may be pretty common for you even though his team was winning the game by a big margin. If you don't know him, you may think that he is on the losing team. Why is that? As he told ESPN:

"I know I get criticized for that. Everybody says, 'He just won 31–3. What's he complaining about?' But it goes back to the inner scoreboard versus the outer scoreboard. Which one is more important? If you're going to accomplish your goals, it's always the inner scoreboard."

He was upset about the little things. It could be because someone didn't follow the play that he planned, or maybe someone was not in their position. It may be the fact that everyone did not perform at their very best.

You may think that these errors should be overlooked when the team is winning, but not for Nick Saban. Even during practice, he wants his players to achieve peak performance.

Saban knew if a player had completed his workouts. He made sure that every single drill was done perfectly. He checked whether his players had followed the dress code. He even had a rule that players could not droop their shoulders even though this was a normal posture after practice when they were exhausted. All of these rules point to one question "How good do you want to be?"

We mentioned earlier how little things can snowball into big things. The first place winner does not win by a mile. More often than not, the second place is only behind by a nose. So, every little thing counts. If you do more things correctly than your opponents, you will eventually come out on top. Saban knew that very well and made sure that every little thing went right. If his team did not execute those small actions properly, they did not deserve to win.

To Saban, the outer scoreboard does not matter. It does not always show what you have done right. Instead, we should all have our own inner scoreboard to keep track of our progress.

Keep Moving Forward

Having a goal alone is not enough. It tells you what you should strive forward, but it does not tell you what you need to do to reach that end. This is why you need a couple of goals with an action plan – the process. It gives you a checklist of items to tick off. That way, you know what the next step is to reach your goal. You know where you are and you are accountable for your actions.

Goals are also relatively short-term. They give you a boost in confidence when you overcome them, but they may cause you to become complacent. If you fail, it is difficult for you to recover and get yourself sorted again.

On the other hand, if you follow a process, you know that there is something you should do. If you miss a workout or make a mistake, you can always aim to get it next time around. The process gears you up toward long-term thinking because it is all about commitment and following a plan over a long time.

Entrepreneur Gary Vaynerchuk often talks about "macro patience, micro speed." This is the spirit behind the process. Nowadays, many of us develop instant gratification thanks to the internet. We become impatient and worry about what will happen in a few years. Yet, we spend our days making poor decisions and wasting our time.

To get our lives sorted, we need to have a process we can follow. DO not become so enamored with your goals that you forget what you should be doing right now. Have a set goal and design a process to achieve it, and then commit to the process. Simply put, do your job.

On Dealing with Anger

How do we become angry? This is a predictable emotion for the Stoics, not unforeseeable mishaps. It is not an automatic response that we cannot control, either. So when someone does something offensive, when they do something harmful, offensive, threatening, or wrong, we will react with anger. We follow a process in which we get angry. Understanding this process, and how it works, can lead us to manage our anger over time.

We can examine our thought process by understanding anger as an emotional and bodily response, not just raw affectivity. There is an underlying thought-process driving it. So, we at least know that this is something we can control. Epictetus said that our work, our choices, desires, denials, assents, judgments, and assumptions are the things that are in our control.

As a rule of thumb, when we get angry, we are wrong in our evaluation of what is happening and in our reasoning about the matter in relation to other things. Simply put, anger results from what we think is good and bad, how we order and value things, and what we desire and are averse to.

If we want to manage and master our own emotions, we need to understand them first. This entails examining what we value, what we think is good and bad, and our own desires. If we can be honest with ourselves, we can assess the situation better and perhaps identify the things that are outside our scope of power. These things are not good or bad per se, but we still treat them as such because we feel they are good or bad. As we have covered in a previous chapter, we should not allow external events to influence our emotions. In this case, we would be wrong in our assumption if we determine something to be good or bad if it is outside our area of control.

By doing so, we make ourselves vulnerable to the world, especially to those who are not rational. As Epictetus pointed out, the only thing you can predict about them is to study their thought process – to learn what seems rational to them but isn't in reality.

But let us not talk about those people, as we cannot control their behavior. What we want to work on is ourselves. How exactly do we get our assumptions wrong in the first place? Of course, it depends on the person in certain situations. Among all of the unique events, there are certain commonalities we can pick out. One of which is the assumption that whatever happened or has been done to us, should not or should never have occurred.

What causes this "should not" assumption in our thought process? At the bottom, it comes from our desire for things to go our way, the things that are outside our control. We want to cling onto things that may possibly be ours, but don't necessarily have to be. We also want others to treat us in certain ways and not in others because we see their actions and words as indicators of what they think and feel about us. Basically, we want a perfect world in which people and events go our way. Of course, this is not the case, so we feel wronged, become angry, and want revenge.

Addressing Anger As It Arises

It is worth developing an understanding of our irrationality, its negative consequences or how it is counterproductive to our lives. For some, these insights might even be needed if they want to control or address their anger. Of course, just by getting a firm grasp of our weak points in our character and our own thought process does not change much.

We can analyze, scrutinize, or reflect on ourselves without really addressing the problem. In fact, we may become complacent and replace practical effort with contemplative work. Epictetus also talked about this, criticizing those who confused studying and putting what they've learned into practice. It is possible to go one step further but it still does not resolve problems. We can make all sorts of plans and resolutions, even complex ones, and still not get very far with keeping our anger under control.

Therefore, the best way to go forward is by doing something about it. When we realize that our emotional response, anger, is detrimental to our peace of mind, we can begin to put in conscious efforts into controlling our emotions. If you recognize that your anger is something that is bad for you and really want to do something about it, then you need to choose some of the most effective means to that end. How effective they are is determined by how much effort you put into practicing them.

We need to remind ourselves that what is at stake is the motivation we all need to deal with our own anger, which is far from a walk in the park. Controlling our own emotions means opposing a part of ourselves that is pressing upon us, messing us up through the process, and dominating how we should think and feel.

If we wish to go on the Stoic path, we need to resist that part of ourselves. So, what can we do to manage our anger? In the book titled "Discourse," Epictetus offered us several concrete actions we can act upon.

Understand Why

As we mentioned earlier, people have a reason for their behavior. The reason is quite understandable as well if we put ourselves in their shoes. While those who anger us often do not think rationally, what they do does seem rational to them. We have different thought processes, emotional responses, desires, etc. so what they think is logical to them may not be so logical to us. If we can understand what they do as partly rational and partly irrational, it will make sense that they act this way. We will then be less bothered by it.

Distancing From the Appearances

Every day, we are faced with all sorts of appearances that tell us how they should be interpreted and played into our network of desires and aversions, assumptions and opinions. We do not have to assent to them automatically, especially to those that upset us. These appearances have to do with harm or insult to ourselves when others want to harm or insult us. So, just see them as events that happen and remain neutral about the whole thing. Again, it is not the outside mishap that upsets us, it is how we perceive and react to it.

Remind Ourselves of Our Humanity

When we fail morally, we resemble a class of animals metaphorically. Anger is associated with beasts of prey, engaging in activities appropriate for their class as animals, but not for us as humans. This is a classic anger management technique. When we liken our reactions to animals, we bring ourselves before our eyes and are, therefore, able to determine what we'd look like when we become angry. At the same time, we can remind ourselves that we are not animals. We are humans who are capable of choosing how we can respond and how we can approach problems rationally.

Removing Ourselves from Competition

If we take what other people see as goods, which are often external (outside our control), to be meaningful and genuine goods, we will be dragged into conflict with others over those goods. We may even experience conflict with ourselves as well because what we believe to be good may not be good to others. When we try to pursue the goods from both perspectives, it can create a rift in ourselves. So, to combat this, we need to remind ourselves that what we are pursuing are external things that do not necessarily make us happy. You do not need to struggle against other people to get it.

Fulfilling Your Roles towards Others

When we get angry at someone and act upon that anger towards them, we normally transgress the role and its associated duties in relation to those people. We have a choice here. We can maintain or restore that role in ourselves. Your roles can be a friend, a citizen, a family member, a neighbor, etc. Restore that role, or give in to anger. It can be hard to remain friends with someone that you are angry with. We can also place our anger on the fact that they failed to fulfill their own roles towards us. This means that your anger stems from their failures, not yours so you can calm yourself down because this is not something you should waste time and energy on. Their failure is outside your control, after all.

Chapter 8: On the Art of Mental Toughness

What do you think determines how far you will go in life? Is it wealth, health, fame, or something else?

This tough question has been asked and answered for ages. Back in the '60s, Stanford professor Walter Mischel conducted the Marshmallow experiment. Here, children had to choose whether they could get one marshmallow right away, or wait a little longer to get two.

Those who decided to wait for two reported doing better in life in general, even forty years later. This ability to delay gratification is also related to higher SAT scores, lower levels of substance abuse, lower likelihood of obesity, and many other indicators of success.

After that, Angela Duckworth documented the results of her research in her book titled "Grit" the following:

- West Point cadets who got the highest score on the Grit Test were 60% more likely to succeed than their peers.
- Ivy League undergraduate students who were mentally tough also had a higher GPA than their peers even though they had lower SAT scores and weren't perceived as "smart."
- When comparing two people who are the same age and have different levels of education, the level of mental toughness (but not intelligence) more accurately determines who will be better educated.

From what we can tell from these studies, we can say with certainty that characteristics such as grit, perseverance, and self-control are key to success. We can put them under the mental toughness umbrella. Therefore, if you want to go far in life, mental toughness is key. So, how do we go about reinforcing our minds?

Deconstruct Things

To start with, you need to remain steadfast, unintimidated by the challenges ahead of you. In many cases, we become paralyzed by the sheer size of the obstacle that we end up throwing our hands up and resigning instead of working to overcome it and reach our goal.

So, when you are faced with an obstacle, the first step would be to deconstruct it into bite-sized chunks. You have to break it down into small actionable steps to allow you to tackle the problem. When you break things down into bite-sized chunks, you can create a process that you can follow to tackle the problem. This allows you to track your own progress, giving you a sense of control, and eventually allowing you to overcome the problem.

When you allow yourself to remain steadfast in the face of an insurmountable obstacle, you create an opportunity for yourself to remain calm and rational so you can assess the situation properly. This is how successful people manage to maintain their peak performance even in stressful situations. They do not capitulate when they have to climb a mountain because they break down the mountain into individual steps. Anyone can take a step forward. These people know how far and how fast they need to climb.

Going up just a meter allows you to chalk up a small victory, giving you the mental strength to go onward. Marathoners have the same mindset. They do not think that they need to run 26 miles. They just focus on their pace and the next landmark. That gives them a more realistic goal to pursue.

Reframe Negative Events

"Men are disturbed not by things, but the view they take of them." – Epictetus

If you didn't know already, life is unfair and it will beat you senseless at certain points. This is something that you cannot change. So, the Stoic approach here is to not worry about what comes your way, but rather prepare yourself mentally on how you want to react to it.

Mentally resilient individuals do not view failure as a knockout punch. Instead, they brush it off as a bruise and continue on ahead. They know that their plan is not without flaws and they expect failures. This is just as good a feedback as success. Failure is not a condemnation of their abilities. It is nothing personal.

In the book "The Startup of You," Reid Hoffman urges people to remain in the state of "permanent beta." Similar to products released for testing, flaws are to be expected. So are you. You cannot expect yourself to be the perfect human being. The path to perfection is long, with success and failures. By putting yourself in this state, you allow yourself space to improve as you expect to encounter a lot of obstacles. You see each failure as feedback from which you can improve quickly. So, you are a work-in-progress.

As Thomas Edison once said, "I have not failed. I've just found 10,000 ways that won't work." This is the view you need to adopt if you want to go far in life. The more you try, the more mistakes you will make. But that is not necessarily a bad thing. Trying and failing is always better than not trying at all. In order to grow and develop, you need to step out of your comfort zone, which involves risks. Mentally strong individuals do not allow themselves to be weighed down by negative mishaps. So shouldn't you. This is not about optimism, either. This wishful thinking alone gives you mental strength, but it will not get you very far.

Acknowledge Your Challenges

Admiral Jim Stockdale was taken prisoner during the Vietnam War. The Viet Cong did not follow any humanitarian treaties, so they treated prisoners as they pleased. You can imagine what they did to him. He was tortured over twenty times during his eight-year imprisonment from 1965 to 1973. He miraculously survived the war even though he had no prisoner's rights, no set release date, and no certainty on whether he would even survive to see his beloved family again.

Still, even when the situation looked grim for him, Stockdale never lost hope. He said that he never doubted the fact that he would get out, and that he would prevail in the end and then turn this horrible experience into the defining experience in his life. This was something he would not trade in retrospect.

So, was this just sheer optimism? This is known as the Stockdale paradox, as he mentioned that it was always the most optimistic prison mates that failed to survive the imprisonment. He said:

> "They were the ones who said, 'We're going to be out by Christmas.' And Christmas would come, and Christmas would go. Then they'd say, 'We're going to be out by Easter.' And Easter would come, and Easter would go. And then Thanksgiving, and then it would be Christmas again. And they died of a broken heart."

This is the Stockdale paradox. Jim Collins noted in his book "Good to Great," self-deception can help you overcome short-term discomfort or embarrassment. However, it is unhealthy in the long run as it will come back to haunt you.

Therefore, pure optimism is not the way to go. You must balance optimism with realism. You need to acknowledge that the difficulties are real and you need to be willing to pay the price. Most of the time, people lose hope because of their unrealistic assessment and expectation of the situation. They become overwhelmed when reality sets in, and they are faced with a sense of helplessness.

"You must never confuse faith that you will prevail in the end — which you cannot afford to lose — with the discipline to confront the most brutal facts of your current reality, whatever they might be." – Jim Stockdale

Find Your Purpose

Angela Duckworth said that grit is the perseverance and passion to achieve a long-term goal. She interviewed those with exceptional grit and noted that every one of them pursues something that has a purpose.

So, what is purpose?

There is no general definition, so it is up to you to define. What we all agree on is that purpose gives you a powerful motivation to succeed even if the odds are stacked against you. It keeps you going even when you are faced with agonizing pain. You keep pushing through the pain because you know the pain of discipline hurts less than the pain of regret. This is the power of purpose.

Purpose does not need to be a big or abstract concept, either. You just need to look to something or someone that you care about. You will find your purpose there.

A soldier may fight hard for his comrade beside him, or for his country. A mother may wake up in the middle of the night because her infant cries, and she may cajole him back to sleep. Activists, though their actions seem insignificant and may not influence major political decisions, still gather around and get as much support as possible to voice their demands. People are willing to work tirelessly if they work toward something that they believe in, no matter the obstacle.

"He who has a why to live can bear almost any how." – Friedrich Nietzsche

Mentally resilient individuals can bear all their trails and errors in their attempt to achieve their goal because they have an intrinsic driving force. As a result, they can remain steadfast and push forward even through difficult times.

Recharge and Recover

While mental resilience often gives you an image of a person weathering all hardships, no one can do it infinitely. A large portion of mental toughness is recovery. After all, we have biological limits to what we can take.

Our mind becomes ineffective if it is put through too much stress over a period of time. Just like your muscles, your willpower can get burnt out eventually. Researchers call this the decision fatigue because every single decision we make reduces our willpower. Here, every little decision counts.

Barack Obama and Mark Zuckerberg are known for the fact that they wear the same clothing every day. They do this to conserve their willpower. As a result, they can make better decisions when a lot of things are at stake.

Shawn Achor and Michelle Gielan argued in their Harvard Business Review that it is all about how you recover, and not how you endure a hard time. They wrote that the key to resilience is doing your best, then pausing, recovering, and then trying again. We need to rest now and again in order to achieve peak performance.

Do not let work drain you of your willpower even when you are not there. Give yourself time to rest, recharge, and be immersed in the moment. This is why mindful practices are critical for mental tranquility.

Whenever you can, get off your social media accounts and emails. These things force you to kind of keep chugging on, which is not going to help you in the long run. When you do this, you do not allow your brain to recover and prepare for the next stressful event because you plug into another source of mental stimulus. So, get enough rest and recover properly.

Mentally resilient individuals ensure that they get enough rest. So, they have enough mental strength to last through even the toughest times. You should strive to do the same if you want to really reinforce your mind.

Flex the Muscle

Mental toughness is a skill, meaning that you can develop it through constant practice and conscious effort. As with anything involving personal growth, you will need to step outside your comfort zone and learn to be comfortable being uncomfortable. This is true when you need to increase your mental resilience since you can only tap into this strength when you are faced with a difficult challenge. Therefore, mental toughness is one of the most critical characteristics to develop.

Navy SEALs adopt the 40% rule that they live by. Basically, when your mind tells you that you are done, you are only 40% done. This is why almost all runners that participate in a marathon finish when most ordinary people stop at mile 16.

This means going the extra mile and pushing yourself through the brutal conditions. Keep taking that one extra step, even if you are out of breath. Are your arms burning? Give yourself one more rep. As Winston Churchill says, "if you're going through hell, keep going."

Many people would've given up when they grew tired, but not you. This gives you an edge in life as well because it shows others that you can succeed where others tend to fail.

Stay Resilient

Life is unfair. It will beat you down to your knees and make sure you stay down if you allow it. To go far ahead in life, you need to strengthen your mind to overcome even the most difficult obstacles and recover from the most painful failures. When you do, you will realize that there is no river too wide or mountain too tall. You can overcome anything.

Chapter 9: Other Practical Tips and Practices

Other than all the other practical advice we have covered, these are some of the tips that do not quite fit in with others.

Add a Reserve Clause – If Nothing Prevents You

"I will sail across the ocean if nothing prevents me." – Seneca

We have mentioned time and again that it is vital that you know that everything is not under your control. You can only do a few things. The Stoics know that well, so they say that they will try to do something, "as long as nothing prevents" them. This reserve clause helps tone down our expectations somewhat and reminds us that there is always uncertainty in the things that we do.

We do not know what tomorrow will bring. As they used to say, come what may. Here, the Stoics take it a step further. They put all of their efforts into doing something, but they know very well that the ultimate outcome is beyond their direct control. They accept this fact, so whatever the result is, they know that they are not to blame. They eliminated the fact that their laziness or carelessness led them to their failure. They did their best, so they have no reason to blame themselves if the outcome does not turn out to be the way they expected.

This exercise works like this: When you are going to do something, add a reserve clause like "God willing," or "if nothing prevents me."

- I'll finish this project today if nothing prevents me.
- See you tomorrow, if nothing happens.
- I'll give voluntary discomfort and go a week without the internet if nothing prevents me.

Love Your Fate

"Fate leads the willing, and drags along the reluctant." – Seneca

While we are on the topic of control, let us talk about fate. People say that we are masters of our own fate, but we do not have as much control over it as we think. The Stoics advised us not to wish for the reality to be any different. Instead, we should all accept and love it as it is. They say that fate is like a moving cart, and we are the dog that is leashed to it.

A foolish man would tug and bite at the leash, fighting the cart as it moves along. In the end, they would still be dragged with the cart anyway, no matter how hard he struggles. On the other hand, a wise man would be in the same situation, but he would run alongside the cart, keeping pace with it.

You cannot change what happens in life, so the best thing to do is to just accept it rather than fight every insignificant thing that happens. We're the dog that is leashed to the cart and the only thing we can control is how close we want to be to that cart. Even that is limited. So, instead of being dragged along, we might as well enjoy the journey.

To resent what happens means that you assume that you have a say in the matter. We do not.

So, whenever something happens to you, ask yourself whether you can do something about it. If yes, then do something about it. If not, then it's not under your control. Its fate, so accept it as it is. There is no point in fighting it because it will only make you look bitter and miserable. You need to adopt these three principles:

- Nonattachment: Everything has its end, so do not get too attached to what you like.

- Nonjudgment: Do not judge the event. It changes nothing. Accept them as they are.
- Nonresistance: Do not wish the reality to be any different.

Forgive the Wrongs of Others

"When a man asserts, then, to what is false, know that he had no wish to assent to the false: 'for no soul is robbed of the truth with its own consent,' as Plato says, but the false seemed to him true." – Epictetus

The Stoics believe that everyone tries to do the right thing, even though it is actually not the case. Most of the time, we do not commit a wrong on purpose. Therefore, we should treat those who misbehave with pity rather than blame.

After all, is it fair for us to be angry at someone when we know that that person doesn't know any better? That is why we need to be tolerant and kind instead. We should learn to forgive others. As Jesus said, "Father, forgive them, for they don't know what they are doing."

So, before you get angry with someone, stop and tell yourself that the person does not know any better. In doing so, you can calm yourself and be kind and forgiving.

- Do not seek revenge when someone wrongs you: It comes from weakness, so be strong and choose to be tolerant and kind instead.
- Pity instead of blame: They are merely blinded by their own mind.
- If someone is being impolite to you, try to see it as a way to train your mind. We all learn and try to become better people. So, this is your chance to train your mental resilience. Shake it off and move on.

Buy Tranquility

"Starting with things of little value – a bit of spilled oil, a little stolen wine – repeat to yourself: 'For such a small price I buy tranquility and peace of mind." – Epictetus

This is what all Stoics strive towards. One of the things they excel at is staying calm even in the face of adversity. No matter what comes his way, he remains calm and collected.

"I buy tranquility instead," is a sentence we should tell ourselves. It can save us a lot of mental energy. When something happens that you do not like and that arouses your anger and excitement, tell yourself, "I buy tranquility instead." Then, move on calmly, with a smile.

Try to incorporate this quote into your life. It will be worth it. Of course, it requires you to be aware of your own emotions and step in between the stimulus and your response. If you can stop the former from reaching the latter, you can benefit from this quote.

So, try to be aware of your life. When something happens that makes you feel discontent or angry, tell yourself, "I buy tranquility instead."

- When you spill some coffee on your clothes – buy tranquility instead.
- When your roommate doesn't do the dishes – buy tranquility instead.
- When the person driving in front of you is going too slow – buy tranquility instead.

16 Lessons for Living

In the thirty-third part of Epictetus' Handbook, you will find plenty of good advice for living a meaningful, happy life. It is the longest part of the Encheiridion and gives an insight into the best practices in a wide range of areas, especially in a social situation. It is a good idea to adopt these lessons, but there is no need to follow every single one of them. It is okay if you disagree with some of them, as these lessons may not be applicable in your situation. These 16 lessons are:

1. Create a type of character and model for yourself that you will follow no matter what.
2. Keep quiet and speak what is required, but sparingly. Only when communication is needed, speak. Again, do not speak about trivialities such as the everyday subjects and especially about other people to blame them, praise them, or compare them.
3. When you can, speak up to lead the conversation to what is proper. If you find yourself in a company that thinks differently, then remain silent.
4. Do not laugh at many things, or much, or without restraint.
5. Never make promises if you can. If not, refuse as far as you can.
6. Do not go to parties hosted by an outsider or a layman. However, if you

find yourself in such a situation, focus your attention and do not get in the way of a layman. If your companion is stained with wine, anyone who rubs against him will be just as dirty if that person happens to be clean himself.

7. For your body, you only need the bare necessities such as food, drink, clothes, and shelter. Reject anything that is for show or for pure luxury.

8. If possible, keep clear of sex before marriage. If you do engage in it, keep it appropriate. Do not provoke or shun anyone that engages in it. Also, do not bring forward the fact that you do not engage in it yourself.

9. If someone tells you that someone else talked about you behind your back, do not defend yourself against the claim. Instead, say that the person must not be aware of your other faults, else he would not have mentioned only what he said.

10. You do not need to go to an award show often. If you go, do not show that you support anyone else except yourself. Only yearn for what happens as it happens, and only that the winner takes the prize. This way, you will not be let down. Stop yourself from shouting or cheering for someone, or getting too excited. After everything ends, do not speak of what happened if it does not lead to your own improvement. Otherwise, others would think that you were captivated by the show.
11. Do not go into someone's presentation so casually or at random. If you must, preserve your dignity and composure as you go, while trying your best to not be a nuisance.
12. When you are about to meet someone, especially a high-ranking individual, think of what Zeno or Socrates would do in your situation. You can never go

wrong by behaving like them in the encounter.

13. When you are about to visit someone with great power, imagine that you will not find him at home, or that you will be shut out, or that his doors will be slammed in your face, or that he will not notice you. With all of this in mind, if you still think that you should visit that person, then think about what may happen during the visit and never tell yourself that it's not worth that much. Doing so is like a fool and someone who is affected by external things.

14. When you are with other people, refrain from describing your own achievements and adventures excessively or frequently. It may be pleasant for you to recall your epic tales, but it is not the case for others who have to listen to you.

15. At the same time, try not to evoke laughter. This can lead quickly to

vulgarity and can cause those around you to lose respect for you.

16. It is risky to use obscene language as well. Whenever someone else uses it, rebuke that person. If that's not possible, try to show your disapproval about their use of language by keeping quiet, blushing, or looking visibly stern.

Chapter 10: Conclusion

That is all you need to know to start your journey down a path of virtue toward mental tranquility and meaningful life. Ancient philosophers have given us much to learn about the idea of Stoicism, and it is highly recommended that you check out their works.

To wrap everything up, there is one more tip worth mentioning. Do not be too harsh on yourself. Living a Stoic life can be difficult for many people as it requires you to detach from material possessions. Try your best to lead a good life and act appropriately in social situations. Follow what the Stoics said. You can never go wrong. At the same time, do not beat yourself up too harshly if you fail to follow one of their teachings. We are all humans, after all. What matters is that you keep up the effort in improving yourself.

With that in mind, good luck with your journey.

www.ingramcontent.com/pod-product-compliance
Lightning Source LLC
Chambersburg PA
CBHW071238070526
44583CB00017B/2237